PRAISE FOR LORI

"In clear, compelling prose, Lori Morrison tells how she entered into a state of spiritual madness following the death of her husband, and of her path back to spiritual wellness. Hers is a remarkable, memorable—and vivid—journey."

—**Robert Whitaker,** *award-winning journalist and author of the New York Times bestseller* Anatomy of an Epidemic *and* Mad in America

"A blow-by-blow account of what happens when a modern woman's comfortable earthly reality is shattered by an explosive awakening to vast unseen dimensions and the haunting call of an ancient Mayan priestly legacy."

—**Cate Montana,** *author of* The E Word *and* Unearthing Venus

"It is remarkable to come to know Lori through her unbelievably heavy spiritual initiation experience. Her story has been transformative for me."

—**Joost Elffers,** *creative producer of the New York Times best-selling* The Secret Language of Birthdays *and author of* Off Planet

"Heart-wrenchingly beautiful, authentic, brave, and compelling, Lori Morrison's memoir had me streaming tears and laughing out loud."

—**Katie Mottram,** *Founding Director, International Spiritual Emergence Network*

"WOW. Like an embodiment of the Phoenix, Morrison describes how, through the ashes of a dismantled life and dying to who she no longer was, she rose up as a healer, sage, and teacher capable of guiding others through similar rites of passage."

—**Kelley Alexander,** *Program Director, Director of Alternative and Complementary Health, and Counselor, The Sanctuary at Sedona*

"This book is an absolute treasure, a rare gift. It should be mandatory reading in every psychology and psychiatry training program. What a trailblazer. What a woman. What a book!"

—**Barbara Glazier-Robinson, Ph.D.,** *psychologist*

LORI

The Disintegration of My Ordinary Reality

Lori Morrison

Four Jaguars Press
Sedona, Arizona

Four Jaguars Press is an imprint of Spirit Concierge LLC
Sedona, Arizona

www.lorimorrison.com

Typographic design by Patricia Childers

Cover design by Joost Elffers

Copy editing by Stephanie Gunning

Special discounts are available on quantity purchases by schools,
associations, and others.

For details, contact the publisher at
bulkorders@lorimorrison.com.

Lori/ Lori Morrison. —1st edition

ISBN 978-0-9987378-0-5

Library of Congress Control Number: 2017902519

I DEDICATE THIS BOOK TO all who have experienced a life-altering experience.

To my husband, Tino, who continues to inspire me with his infinite love, wit, and practical wisdom from "the other side."

To my cats, Footsie, Toe, and Canela, and my German shepherds, Bruno and Baco, who kept the light on at the end of the tunnel for me.

"You shall see it coming from afar.

The beam comes to awaken us.

It comes to us from everywhere."

From the book of *Chilam Balam*
of Chumayel,
a fifteenth–century jaguar priest

In the indigenous cultures of Central America, what western medicine terms a mental illness is understood as signaling the birth of a healer or shaman. Mental disorders are viewed as spiritual emergencies that require support from sages in the community who understand the connection we have to the spirit realm. A problem in the developed world is that we are not taught about the possibility that psychic phenomena exist. In fact, people who profess that they have psychic abilities too strongly—with the exception of a few celebrity psychics on TV—are generally considered crazy. Hearing voices and perceiving other people's thoughts can be diagnosable conditions.

A shaman walks the thin line of insanity and bliss. There is nothing casual about how this calling presents itself. Those who become shamans must make a sacrifice—they have no choice about it. The mind must be rewired in order to find the soul. This often initiates a mental crisis. When spiritual energy enters someone ill-equipped to deal with it, the outcome can be so chaotic that the individual is deemed psychotic. When drugs are administered in such situations, the problem can become even more severe since drugs may mask the reality of what is happening. This is what happened to me several years ago following the death of my husband of twenty-three years.

Lori Morrison
May 2017

CHAPTER ONE

DURING THE RAINY SEASON IN EL SALVADOR, Lake Ilopango turns emerald green. Waterfalls tumble into the jungle and lush vegetation cascades down the walls of the caldera that was formed after a volcanic eruption many centuries ago. I am still in awe of how powerful the explosion of lava must have been that blasted open the earth and created this deep and legendary crater lake. Ilopango is a paradise and the place that holds the fondest memories for me of my husband, Tino. We spent hours there on our pontoon boat.

On the last day of Tino's life, I lowered the speed of the motorboat as we arrived at the dock below the high peninsula where we'd built our home. Tino's best friend, Bobby, and his girlfriend, Annie, were with us. We had taken a fun ride around the lake and were now hungry for lunch. Annie and I were the first on board the small tram that led up the cliff to the house. At the top we waited for Bobby and our caretaker, Edgardo, to help Tino onto the tram for the next trip since he had trouble walking. We had plans to eat lunch poolside. We'd open a bottle of wine and Tino would have some vodka with fresh coconut water.

When the tram arrived carrying Tino and Bobby, I could see that Tino was not himself. I asked him what was wrong and his eyes flashed with fear as he tried to speak. His mouth moved, but he was struggling to make words come out. I moved closer to him to better hear the sounds from his trembling lips and I could barely make out, "Lori, I can't talk!" There had been many close calls before, but none like this.

For a moment I stood there, powerlessly watching Tino struggle as his life energy was dissipating. I snapped to, seeing I needed to get him medical attention. Bobby and I managed to get Tino to the driveway and into the car, and as soon as he sat down his head fell back limply on the neck support. There was a second of deafening silence and then both his arms reached up—up as if he was grabbing for the hands of someone who had arrived to take him away.

Tino was diagnosed with diabetes shortly before we were married. Although the disease slowly eroded his body's ability to sustain itself, I had always pictured his death as a dramatic scene of a bedside farewell with someone reading bible verses over the soft cries of friends and family. Instead, for thirty desperate minutes I fought to revive the body of the man who had become my entire world. I was going to fix this. The thought, *Nobody is going to check out on my watch!* roared through my mind as I ran for the portable defibrillator.

Our house was a virtual emergency room, with closets full of every imaginable product to heal wounds and any other health challenge that might be thrown our way. I was prepared for anything and felt certain that, just like so many times before, this incident would be a temporary setback. I placed the sticky patches of the defibrillator on Tino's chest and with panicked confidence I pushed the START button and waited.

"Do not engage," said the computer-generated voice of the device.

I frantically pushed the button again and again, but continued to hear "Do not engage." My eyes finally focused on the screen to see no flickers and no bleeps—just a steadily moving flat line. I threw the machine on the gravel and started CPR.

Over and over, I pressed my will into his rib cage. I sent every breath of life I had into his lungs, which moved up and down. After every few breaths I would raise Tino's eyelids with the hopes of seeing the sparkle in his eyes that had brought so much joy to my life, but something was missing. I felt I could not give up trying to revive him, hoping that some miracle was on the horizon.

Annie, who stood helplessly near me, finally put her arm on my shoulder and said, "Lori, you've done all you can. Tino is gone."

These words stung like hot poison darts, piercing every inch of my being. I got out of the car and staggered across the gravel, almost collapsing from the searing pain of my failure and loss.

The entire household had assembled in the driveway: Maria and Carmen, our housekeepers for so many years; Jorge, the gardener; Edgardo, our caretaker; and Bobby and Annie. All of us were standing together in a circle of stunned disbelief. I looked at the faces of our two sweet German shepherds, Baco and Bruno, lying near the car with their heads on their paws. Their soft eyes gazed at me for answers I could not provide. I then looked back at Tino's body, which was now merely a mass of flesh. I realized I was no longer looking at Tino. My efforts to ensure my husband's survival were over.

I told the maids and gardener to go get the teak chaise longue and then we all lifted Tino's lifeless body out of the car, placed it onto the chaise, and carried it into the nearest room in the guesthouse.

The lake house was in a remote area without the easiest access. Because it was a holiday, it would take a while for the coroner to arrive. I planned to stay next to Tino until the coroner came. All I could see was a body and betrayal. The body had won, while I had lost the battle for his survival. All my efforts over the past five years to keep Tino alive were going to be buried with him. There would be nothing to show for the constant care, for the weeping I did in hospital waiting rooms as every few months another toe was amputated, more cancerous tumors were removed from his lungs, or a major artery was cleared with a stent. The entire effort had been lost to the inevitable process of death.

I was a failure. What did I miss? What could I have done differently to avoid this? After all the effort, all I was left with was dead silence.

Eventually, I stood up and numbly began walking out of the guesthouse in total defeat. But as I was leaving, I heard Tino's voice. Ever so clearly, he said, "Lori, I am not there." My head jerked in the direction of his body. For a second I thought that the whole scene was just a nightmare. A mistake. But he was certainly dead.

I slowly walked through the main house, gazing at what was "us." Everything there was us. After numbly phoning Tino's four daughters who lived in Arizona to give them the sad news, I sat in a daze. By then some other family members had arrived and when I looked at their faces I was hoping to find assurances that somehow this could be fixed. My heart felt shattered. It was as if there was a hole in my chest.

Soon a very strange movement of energy started growing in the area around my heart. At first I thought I might be suffering a heart attack, but the feeling was soft and flowing, and somehow calming. I held my chest as the feeling turned to a warm essence that began to fill the hole that had been blasted open in my heart by the sudden immense grief of losing my beloved husband of twenty-three years. The sensation was powerful and I kept a hand on my chest to protect the movement of this strange flow of energetic matter as it poured into the gaps it met.

The energy pouring into me was so very familiar. It was Tino.

I returned to the guesthouse after a while and stood in the doorway, gazing again at Tino's body, but there was absolutely no attachment to it for me anymore. Nothing. I turned and walked back to the main house, as if seeing Tino lying there somehow contradicted what was suddenly new and alive within me.

For a moment, I experienced a strange euphoria of no longer having to face Tino's daily struggle of living inside a body that had grown incapable of wholeness and health. I wrestled with the release I was sensing, as it seemed such a contradictory emotion to feel at the time of his death. I feared that my indifference toward his body would be misunderstood by friends and family as a lack of sympathy, but there was no way to avoid the intensity of what I was feeling. It was the greatest sense of freedom I have ever felt.

This was not any kind of freedom from the need to care for Tino. Rather it was the sharing of Tino's freedom from the pain of connection to an improperly functioning body. Later I would come to realize that Tino and I were both feeling the relief of the separation of his soul from his body, as well as its liberation from the density of where it had been.

CHAPTER TWO

I WAS INTRODUCED TO TINO in Scottsdale, Arizona, when he was looking for a real estate agent. Tall, dark, and handsome, six-foot-two-inches tall, and with perfectly coifed gray hair, this suave Salvadoran had moved to the United States in the late 1970s to keep his family safe from the violence that was occurring in his homeland. After being invited to some social gatherings he also attended, I realized that his trademark was the way he held a crystal tumbler of Johnny Walker Black on the rocks between his thumb and third finger while telling one of his captivatingly funny stories.

There was always a celebration of life around Tino. He could change the entire energy in a room with his presence. It was easy to know when Tino had left a room, as his energy was so bountiful and generous. He thrived on being around people and had the ability to make everyone at every level of society feel comfortable around him. There were no barriers between Tino and others. Tino was about spreading laughter, mostly by making fun of the whimsy of life.

Tino was the most honest and fair person I have ever met. In all the time I knew him, Tino never spoke an unkind word about anyone including his three ex-wives. He could be judgmental, especially with his family, but the judgment was firm and fair, as deep inside it came with compassion for their circumstances and who they were. Although, to be frank, Tino had quite an ego, it was fueled by the love and adoration of those around him who recognized his charismatic charm.

The aforementioned characteristics allowed Tino to excel both in society and in business. He was a generator of positive energy, which sparked many successful endeavors and partnerships, and he was generous to those who understood him. He was adept at living the good life.

Our lives came to an intimate intersection when Tino's third marriage failed and I was widowed at age twenty-seven when my first husband committed suicide. Tino was happy to have found a doubles partner for tennis and I also became his go-to realtor to find him a house after the divorce. After a few months of house hunting and tennis matches, I could sense his desire for something more than a professional relationship.

Although I took time in the beginning to evaluate the possibility of making a life together, I believe we both had an inner knowing that something foundational and profound existed between us. Not entirely convinced, I did, however, agree to move in with him and "give it a try." We settled in the very house that I had found for him a year earlier at the foot of Camelback Mountain in Paradise Valley, Arizona.

After having full-time housekeepers his whole life, Tino was determined that our domesticated relationship would be different. He wanted to live like an American husband and help with the chores. The initial deal we made was that I would cook and he would do the dishes. The first morning all went well. I left him loading the dishwasher. But when I returned to the kitchen an hour later, bubbles pouring from the dishwasher had covered the kitchen floor. A "bubble blob" was even moving well into the family room!

I whooshed away the bubbles and stormed into his office. A brilliant and resourceful civil engineer, he jumped into action with a vacuum cleaner. As he tried to suck up all the bubbles, I watched him with doubts swirling in my head about how this arrangement was ever going to work.

During our first Christmas together, Tino was like a kid. As I was cooking and getting everything ready, I sent him on his only errand—to buy liquor—and he convinced the shop owner to sell him the moving Santa Claus display from the top of the stack of Johnny Walker whiskey cases. When he got home, he happily set it up, so there was Santa with a small bag of gifts slung over his arm, waving his arm back and forth at me from the family room! This was life with Tino: unpredictable, funny, and spontaneous.

A year after we started living together we were having coffee one morning when he very casually said, "I think we need to get married." At that moment I was taking a sip of coffee that I spewed on the breakfast table. "What brought that on?" I asked. Tino replied, "I just think that if I can convince you to come back to El Salvador with me we should be married. You will be giving up a lot for me to go there and I want you to feel comfortable with your emotional and financial investment in our new life together."

That was Tino, fair and wanting always to do the right thing.

After cleaning up the coffee I'd spit on the table, I told him I needed more time. We both had fears of a less-than-happy outcome considering our past experiences with relationships. I think I struggled with it even more, mostly because of the twenty-five-year age difference we had, which made him older than my father—even though with Tino's childlike character I often felt much wiser than him. Since I was falling madly in love with Tino I knew that to really know all of Tino I would need to know Central America as well. It was time to take our first trip.

It was the spring of 1987, a period when Central America was swarming with communist guerrillas fighting to overthrow several fragile governments that were trying to establish democracies. El Salvador was a war zone whose turmoil was spilling over into the neighboring countries. We would be flying first to Honduras to visit one of his five daughters, who was getting married.

It was around midnight in Houston when we arrived for our flight, and there were a lot of people waiting. Since we were traveling on a 727, I was not sure how all of them were going to fit. Scattered throughout the waiting area were swarms of family members: mothers, fathers, sisters, brothers, grandparents, aunts, uncles, cousins, and friends traveling together. Almost every passenger had a large stereo boombox on his lap, and people's carryons looked like suitcases. Babies were crawling on the carpet crying, cranky because they were up way past their bedtimes. Mothers were yanking the arms of their kids, trying to minimize the chaos. Everyone was speaking Spanish. It seemed that they had all bought hot dogs and bottles of cola were straddled between their thighs.

The Pan Am staff seemed totally outmanned. They had organized stanchions with retractable belt posts for crowd control. As we heard the first call to board, everyone got up and started hugging, crying, and sharing their final words of advice and instructions with their relatives. When Tino and

I reached the entrance to show our tickets, the gate agent was noticeably overwhelmed by it all. When he saw us, there was a little bit of normalcy.

Tino said, "Geez, I am feeling bad that nobody came to say goodbye to me and give me a hug."

Hearing this, the agent smiled and flung his arms around Tino's chest, saying, "There, do you feel better now?"

We boarded and took cover while boomboxes were stuffed into overhead bins.

During the flight to Tegucigalpa, Tino casually mentioned that this would be his first trip to Honduras in many years. There had been a war between El Salvador and Honduras in 1969, and since that time there was an order of capture for Tino by the Honduran government for some "stuff" that had happened in the war. The explanation was sketchy at best and I sensed that he did not want to worry me over the details. What I did understand was that he had been a civilian pilot at that time and the Salvadoran military had the right to force all pilots into the air force if the country was ever at war. This resulted in him becoming an air bomber and running sorties over the capital of Honduras, including dropping bombs on the very airport where we were going to land. He told me the story, very proud of his military service.

I asked Tino what kind of plane he had flown in the war and he said, "My twin-engine plane, which I retrofitted with a chute for dropping bombs." I started to laugh at the thought of this. He then smiled and said that the whole thing was also "complicated" because his wife at the time was Honduran. He shared his standard joke that the only target he was sorry he ever missed was his ex-mother-in-law's house.

The flight attendant stopped by to tell us that our arrival would be delayed since a more important plane, one carrying U.S. Secretary of State George Shultz, was also circling the airport, which would keep us in a holding pattern until he landed. It was not surprising that the Secretary of State was visiting Honduras since the U.S. government was using a base there to aid in the prevention of a communist takeover of Central America. It was widely known that Fidel Castro had expansionist ideas throughout the region. After one of his public speeches he had bragged that he would have breakfast in Nicaragua, lunch in El Salvador, and dinner in Guatemala soon. Breakfast had been assured with Daniel Ortega in Nicaragua, and he was now working on his lunch reservations in El Salvador.

Our pilot was finally given permission to land. I grabbed the sides of my chair, took a deep breath, heard the wheels hit the ground, and we came to a stop. The masses on the plane clapped in joy and relief that we had arrived.

CHAPTER THREE

THE SUN WAS JUST coming up as I stepped out of the plane onto an aluminum stairway that had been rolled up to the door. We walked outdoors toward what looked like an old warehouse, which was the international airport's one and only terminal. Inside were plywood partitions and the whole place had a really bad paint job.

The terminal was hot and humid and without air conditioning, and I was feeling nervous as personal space was at a premium. I said to myself, *Well, Lori, you're not in Kansas anymore.* The native Hondurans are short in stature. Tino at six-foot-two and even I, at five-eight, towered over everyone there. I felt vulnerable with everyone speaking Spanish and knew that I would be relying entirely on Tino, the ex-combat bomber of the Tegucigalpa Airport we were standing in, for everything.

Tino seemed very confident as he chatted with the customs officials. He had insisted to me that the problem with the Honduran government had been cleared up. But there was an array of security forces there with automatic weapons, so I was hoping he was right.

We displayed our passports and since there were no computers, the customs official started to flip through a large book and slowly write down our names and passport numbers. Our passports were then stamped and we were in, with no mention of Tino's earlier wartime escapades.

In the baggage claim area, I looked around for the moving snakelike machines that normally bring bags around in airports, but there were none. We maneuvered into a sea of passengers who were standing in front of a simple door that led out to the tarmac. Every few minutes some young men would enter the door and slide overweight bags into the area of the waiting crowd. Everyone would push and shove to see whether the bags were theirs, and if so, the lucky owners would have to force open a narrow passage to escape the mob. Suitcases and duffle bags were followed by an eternity of boxes, pampers, televisions, boomboxes, microwaves, and baby furniture. I looked with amazement as a toddler's motorized four-wheel jeep went sliding by me. Suitcases were stuffed to their last corner, with bulging zippers.

Most of the women in the crowd were short and stocky. They wore rayon dresses with vinyl shoes. They were dragging their luggage to the inspection table. Customs officials seemed to bask in the power of their position. The lady in front of us presented her bags to the official in front of her, who unzipped the first of four duffle bags. Panties, baby clothes, bras, candies, packs of food, and mysteriously wrapped packages escaped from the opened zipper. Her belongings began piling out of the suitcase like ground sausage bursting from its casing. The official looked a bit leery of going any further with the inspection and instead did his best to help her smash everything that had burst out back into the bag, whereupon she miraculously closed the zipper.

We were next. As the customs agent unzipped our bag, my lacy black bra was the first thing to come flying out. A carefully packed stack of Tino's underwear lay on the table like dominos. My white silk nightgown then slithered out along with a bunch of cigarette cartons, bottles of Johnny Walker Black, and some California Chardonnay. I panicked, thinking that we had probably far exceeded the customs limits. But then Tino "accidentally" caused a $20 bill to fall into the hand of the official and we were waved on our way.

We were finally in Tegucigalpa! A beat-up taxi took us to the only presidential suite in the entire country, which was in the hotel where his daughter's civil wedding would take place.

It is appropriate that my first memory of Central America is of baggage, as this was something Tino had a lot of. Tino had been married and divorced three times, and had five daughters from the first two marriages and two stepchildren who came along with the third marriage. Two of his daughters were older than me. I was only twenty-eight. There were also five sons-in-law and numerous nieces and nephews of different ages whom he had helped raise at different times. So there were plenty of ex-wives, ex-brothers-in-law, ex-sisters-in-law, and ex-mothers-in-law spread around. The only thing he did not have was a cat, which was something he finally got when he met me.

Leaving Tegucigalpa was the same disorganized mess as arrival.

On the flight to El Salvador, I mulled over my reservations about our personal security while we would be there. How safe or unsafe were we? As the plane began its descent, we flew over the sparkling waters of the Pacific Ocean and then passed over a very flat coastal area. Tino looked out the window and was saddened to see that the land below was no longer being cultivated. Until recently El Salvador had been one of the most productive agricultural countries in Central America, but now, due to the complexities of the war and a failed agrarian reform system, the fields that were normally planted with bananas, rice, corn, beans, and sugar cane were barren.

The airport in El Salvador was much more modern than the one in Honduras. Tino absolutely blossomed as he got off the plane, patting folks on the back, seeming to know everyone though not knowing anyone's name. We stopped at the duty-free store where all the staff came out from behind the counter to say hello. It was obvious he was known as a good customer since, without asking, gallons of Johnny Walker appeared and were packed for his purchase. Customs was a breeze as everyone was happy to see Tino. The officials welcomed him back while they quickly slid our bags across the table.

I sensed Tino's happy-go-lucky attitude now that we were in El Salvador, potential security problems and all. Tino's driver, Alonso, pulled up in a bullet-proof Chevrolet Suburban. It was stifling hot outside. I hopped into the back seat and welcomed the air conditioning blowing out of the vents. Tino proudly pointed out the features of the van by showing me holes in the sides of the doors where guns could stick out so that we could shoot at people if they attacked us.

It was *Semana Santa,* or Holy Week, Easter break for the whole country. This takes place in April during the dry season, which lasts from November to May. The topography I saw as we drove to Tino's house was mountainous. The terrain was dry except for areas underneath large conacaste trees that dotted the hillsides and provided shade. We passed piles of coconuts on the side of the road whose vendors lay in hammocks waiting for thirsty clients to stop and buy fresh coconut water.

The capital, San Salvador, was a forty-minute drive from the airport. I was very excited to see Tino's home there. We saw a noticeable presence of armed men along the road we traveled. When I mentioned it to Tino, he said, "No worries, they are the army." He said not to worry about the guerrillas that week, because they, like the military, would take a vacation from the war for Easter. I had a funny vision of leftist guerillas at the beach wearing Che Guevara speedos while carrying AK-47s.

Along the way, I noticed houses vicariously clinging to the edges of ditches and gullies. Many of the homes were simple cardboard constructions with aluminum roofing, patched together with wires and ropes. The mood shifted in the car as we both took in everything we saw. I felt a deep sense of empathy for those who had been reduced to living in such a marginal state after a recent earthquake.

All of sudden, white smoke started spewing out of the engine of the car and we came to a grinding halt by the side of the road. Now I was frightened. Tino began speaking to Alonso in Spanish, and for the next ten minutes I heard the word *puta* ("whore") spewing repeatedly from Tino's mouth. Tino loved this curse word, and it seemed to be serving him well for the predicament we were in. He used it to describe the *puta* car, the *puta* engine, the *puta* fan belt that had busted—all in all, the *puta problema*.

Tino, frustrated and disgusted by now, saw me in the car, and said, "For god's sake, Lori, get out of there. You are cooking like a chicken in a pot!"

I answered, "Don't worry, Tino, I am just fine." Lying. "it is not that hot," just as my body felt about to burst into flames. I was not planning on leaving the bullet-proof Suburban unless I was forced.

I continued to watch the two men contemplating our situation. Tino's hands went from his hips to flying all over the place as if doing that would bring about a solution to this matter. Finally, I could not stand the heat any longer and opened the back door and the front door and stood between them, hoping the guerillas would not take a side shot. "So," I asked Tino, "What exactly is the plan to get us out of here?"

He snapped back at me, saying that we had to hope someone would pick us up since the radio was not working. It was not yet the era of cell phones, so calling for a tow truck was not possible. He wasn't very hopeful that someone would stop. Due to the ongoing civil war, in a crisis it often was every man for himself.

Tino stuck out his thumb and began hitchhiking without luck. A half hour passed before a red minivan finally stopped. After quick negotiations in Spanish that I could not follow, I found myself sitting on a stack of boxes in the back of the van and we were once again on our way to San Salvador.

We turned off the main road and drove through a rather rundown part of town. I was getting concerned that my expectations were not going to be met. I tried to reason with myself and thought that since Tino had been living in the United States for several years perhaps the neighborhood had suffered and his home had become a fixer upper. I was contemplating plan B, which would be to get a hotel room.

My disappointed thoughts were interrupted when the driver got out and slid open the door, which I presumed was to allow me to get out. Much to my relief, after I got out he picked up a box and headed for the door. The driver rang the doorbell, a man appeared and grabbed the box, and then the driver returned to the minivan and we left. Relieved, I asked Tino, "So that was not your house"? He laughed, "No, Lori, the deal I cut with this guy was he would take us home after he made all of his deliveries."

Turning into our neighborhood some while later, I took a deep breath. There were well-groomed gardens and sidewalks with mature trees everywhere I looked. All the properties had brick walls so I could not see the homes behind them.

A garage door opened to a 1960's style ranch house with a woman standing at the front door in a colorful polyester dress and an apron. Tino introduced her as Reina. Three young children peeked out from the side of the house. I waved and they quickly ran away. Tino's house was a welcome relief after our previous stops. The garden was beautiful with a large shade tree and tropical plants everywhere. It held avocado, macadamia, and mango trees and a serene swimming pool. The sound of doves cooing soothed my anxiety. In minutes, I felt safe and relaxed.

When Tino gave me a tour of the house, our last stop was the kitchen. I was surprised to find a rooster walking around the kitchen with his leg tied to one of the cabinet pulls. Reina proudly pointed to him and then to her mouth, illustrating that he would be our dinner that night. I had never known or been introduced to any animal that I was going to eat, so this caused me great consternation. I told Tino that I only eat meat that comes wrapped in white Styrofoam containers with a bar code on it. He ignored the seriousness of my concern and instead put his arm around me, feeling excited to have Reina prepare his favorite dish, *gallo en chicha*. This recipe is prepared by finding a tough fighting cock and soaking it in Mayan liquor made from fermented pineapple and corn. The murdered rooster is soaked all day in the concoction to soften its meat. The dish sort of reminded me of *coq au vin,* but I was far from a Paris bistro.

Later that evening, Tino and I sat at a long dining room table, each of us at opposite ends, and me with a crystal bell next to my water glass. He was evidently proud of Reina's meal as she entered with a large soup tureen and placed it on the table. I watched as Tino enthusiastically scooped out the sweet, thick stock and put chunks of my "pet" rooster into his bowl. But I was struggling with the whole thing and asked if there was any such thing as a tuna sandwich in El Salvador that I could eat instead. Reina went back to the kitchen and happily brought out some tortillas and cheese and an enormous avocado, which became my dinner. I could sense Tino's disappointment with my choice and concern about me assimilating into his culture.

The Salvadoran customs were going to take some getting used to.

That first meal was the most memorable meal I ever had in El Salvador, even though I never took a bite of the main dish.

The week in El Salvador was eye opening. I was glad to see how happy Tino was there. It was obvious that he was popular, loved by his friends and the center of attention wherever we went.

I loved this adventure into the politics, the parties, and the beautiful beaches, lakes, and volcanos that were a backdrop to all the bursting Latin culture and conflict.

CHAPTER FOUR

A FEW MONTHS PASSED AFTER the trip to El Salvador. Then, over breakfast one morning, I finally said yes, I would marry Tino. He was ready to go to City Hall right then and sign the papers. Very practical. I however, wanted our wedding to be something more special than that, so I could enjoy remembering the event in years to come. In the end, we flew to Roatan, a remote island in the southern Caribbean.

Yolanda, the bartender at the small resort where we stayed, was my maid of honor, and sweet Joel, the bellboy with a beaming smile, was Tino's best man. The ceremony took place on a wooden balcony overlooking the serene turquoise waters of the Caribbean Sea. It was a spectacular sight. After the local mayor pronounced us man and wife, a very noisy flock of colorful macaws circled us and settled on the railings around us.

After the honeymoon, I left my job in real estate and we flew to El Salvador to begin our married life there.

Our first fifteen years together were true bliss, and as the years went by we cultivated a successful marriage. On the flip side, in the beginning we were living in a war zone, which led me to experience a string of traumatic events. So although idyllic at times, being with Tino in El Salvador was like tasting the bitter with the sweet.

After settling in El Salvador after our wedding, Tino immediately understood that I would not be happy managing staff at the house, which was the typical plan of most of the women he knew. I was well educated and had enjoyed my previous career working for a New York-based bank financing oil field equipment and million-dollar crude oil shipments for international companies, pampering Saudi princesses who had bulging bank accounts, and managing the investments of corrupt oil company executives and high-ranking military personnel from Mexico and Venezuela. I later worked in international marketing for Robert Mondavi Winery, holding a position that spurred my interest in fine wine and gourmet food.

After the war ended and there was a more pro-business climate in El Salvador, my entrepreneurial blood began flowing through my veins. Over the subsequent decade, I created a significant food and wine business and prominently branded myself as a gourmet food and wine "guru" throughout Central America. Well known, I appeared as a guest on numerous morning TV shows and became an importer to El Salvador of some of the world's most prestigious wines. My reputation afforded me the opportunity to dine with the CEO of the Rothschild family from France, to seek weight-loss advice from chef Julia Child, to get lost in the Marchesi de Frescolbaldi's castle in Montalcino, Italy, to dine in a cave with Miguel Torres, an iconic Spanish winemaker, and to eat cake with renowned vintner Robert Mondavi at his ninetieth birthday party on the Orient Express. At one time, after being awarded several U.S. government food contracts, I was feeding almost 1,500 people a day. In time, I became the ultimate party planner. I was always at the ready to ensure there were drinks flowing and the right wine with the right meal for whoever showed up in our lives.

All along the way, Tino was my cheerleader and the perfect host. Tino spent his time on my personal board of directors as I navigated the unpredictable world of doing business in Latin America. Over time though, Tino's battle with diabetes gradually began to take center stage in our lives, and I know now that the attachment I had to him was deeply rooted in my own pain at witnessing his suffering. I took on his health battles as my own, as together we faced the despair of watching his body disintegrate day by painful day.

The last five years of Tino's life were the most challenging. In this period, I sold the businesses I had started so I could dedicate myself to taking care of the large, gaping diabetic wounds he had on his feet that would never heal. I did research on the internet and tried every form of ointment, injection, and drug possible to heal them. I carefully watched the doctors and nurses as they did wound care and learned how to debride Tino's wounds myself. I even performed small surgeries to remove layers of skin that were impeding the healing process. The head neurosurgeon trying to save his feet at the Mayo Clinic in Scottsdale, Arizona, where we were "frequent flyers," had so much confidence in my ability to take care of Tino's wounds that he would turn a cheek when I opened up the drawers in the examining room. I would hurriedly stock up on disposable scalpels and other instruments, cramming them in my purse to take home with us.

Tino was hospitalized several times due to MRSA infections. As I had become an expert at applying the dressings to his wounds, I would dismiss any efforts from the wound-care nurses since actually I was far better at wound care than they were. Although I had never given a thought to being a nurse, when it came to Tino, a natural sense of how to heal him came through me and I was obsessed with his care.

Because of my research on wound care, we went so far as to send Tino to a Cuban hospital where he received daily injections of a "miracle drug" for three weeks, a treatment that was very successful. Although the doctors at the Mayo Clinic did not advocate for any of our adventures with alternative therapies, they were forced to accept that the wounds had not progressed as they expected—to the point of requiring a full amputation—due to the care I was providing.

Things began to spiral out of control during a trip to New England after my fiftieth birthday. While visiting a romantic seaside village in Maine, we decided to take a short walk back to our hotel room from the restaurant where we had dined. Just as we arrived at our room, Tino collapsed in the entryway. Since he recovered fairly quickly we did not go to the hospital, feeling the collapse was only something minor to do with his blood sugar levels. We arrived at our next stop at a hotel in Vermont, but I couldn't sleep, as I was worried about the slurred speech he had at dinner, so I slipped out of the room in the wee hours of the morning and went to the hotel's business internet center. There, I logged on to the computer and researched several hospitals in New York City. I had decided I was going to take Tino to one of them as soon as possible.

In the morning, Tino woke up and was still not connecting the dots. He was becoming more and more detached from our conversations. I checked his foot, as I did every day, and saw that his big toe was turning blue. This was definitely an emergency situation.

Taking him to a small nearby hospital was out of the question since his health records were as thick as an intricate novel, as he always required very specialized care. I packed up the car and him and set the GPS for New York Presbyterian Hospital in Manhattan. I bought the morning's newspaper and told him to read it to me out loud all the way to New York so that I knew he was remaining coherent along the way.

We entered the chaos of a New York emergency room and we were lucky even to find a gurney. I spent three days in a hallway waiting for a permanent room and begging for the staff's attention as every day another toe would turn blue. This was especially troubling since he had already lost half of his other foot. Thus began a three-month health care odyssey. In reflection, this was the beginning of the end.

On that occasion, Tino lost half of his right foot, as the doctors could not control the infection. His collapse in Maine was diagnosed as a stroke. He needed carotid artery surgery, twice. While doing the pre-op tests for surgery, they found a cancerous tumor in his lung that had to biopsied and later removed.

After three months in New York, I had been in a surgery waiting room five times, pacing and praying alone for news that my husband was still alive, and I had reached the depths of physical and mental exhaustion.

The glimmer in an otherwise desperate string of bad news was Tino, of course. Every week he was honored by the nurse's station as Patient of the Week. His humor about his dilemma pervaded and detracted from the sadness that surrounded the plight of so many patients around us. His incessant negotiations for Haagen Dazs ice cream, pastrami sandwiches, and street vendor hot dogs were legendary among the staff. Every morning's visit by the medical team was met with Tino's jokes and laughter as they reviewed the results of his copious tests. Then they would give us their "diagnosis of the day" —generally more bad news.

Tino ignored it. The day we heard the word *cancer* was especially hard on me. I looked to Tino for his reaction, but he completely ignored what had been said and instead pointed at his two cut-off feet and asked the head surgeon to address the prognosis of being able to play golf, while bragging that when the first foot was cut in half he was able to correct a severe left hook on his golf swing that had plagued him for years!

The surgeon and six interns who followed the doctor around put their heads down and tried to disguise the smiles that were triggered by his reaction, which seemed out of place for a topic that was so somber. When they all left the room, Tino turned to me and said, "What is their problem today? They all seem so uptight!"

"Well, Tino," I said, "they just told you that you have cancer, so they probably thought it was not appropriate to laugh at your jokes."

After five surgeries, Tino was finally able to move into an apartment that I had rented for us. With daily nurse visits and the bad news veiling my hopes, the seriousness of his condition was chiseling away at his optimism and taking its toll on both of us.

I had just finished bathing him and getting him dressed, setting up the wound vacuum machine, which sealed the exposed tissue and over time would help pull the skin over the wound on his now half foot, and moving him from place to place to keep the weight off his feet. Tino sat on the edge of the bed with his head down and his shoulders slumped. "Lori, I really don't want to work at staying alive anymore. It takes all I have, so I really have nothing left for me. I no longer have the energy to be alive."

I slowly sat down in the chair across from him, shocked. Tino had never lacked optimism about anything. But his persona had taken a nosedive and the deepest part of Tino's soul was talking to me. It then became my turn to ignore and deny what I was hearing. I steadied my response so as not to reveal my desperation. I spoke curtly and told him how dare he want to give up and how unfair it was to me for him to quit.

At that moment, for the first time in years, it was all about me. I was tallying up the struggle and sizing up the large emotional investment I had in seeing that he got better. I found it unacceptable to appease his desire not to keep trying. The truth was that I could not bear the thought of losing him, so I convinced him to rally—if not for him, then for me—because I could not accept anything less than him being alive.

A few weeks later I was getting Tino ready for what we hoped would be our last trip to Presbyterian Hospital. As usual, our loyal driver, Tony, waited downstairs to take us to the appointments. We were trusting that we would get the green light from the doctors to be able, finally, to go home. We drove down New York's clogged streets again to the hospital.

I wheeled Tino past the doorman and into the bustling energy of the hospital lobby. I'd come to realize that the hospital had approximately 2,000 people going in and out of its doors every day. It was like a small city, and I knew every inch of the place by heart by then. We left our last appointment feeling thrilled because this long and tragic "vacation" was over. Even though Tino was still hooked up with portable tubes and machines and probably would be confined to a wheelchair now, I was optimistic that we were on the road to recovery. Soon we'd be on the plane home to El Salvador.

The next day, I gladly started packing. I picked up Tino's shoes and realized that they would no longer be needed, which meant I would be pushing his wheelchair until his foot healed. I shook my head in sadness while tossing his size thirteen shoes in the garbage. I continued to pack up the summer clothing we had started the trip with and the few warm clothes we had acquired to cope with the chilly fall air in New York. With tears in his eyes, Tony hauled the suitcases down to the car.

As we were leaving New York, I recalled all the leaves, so green and shiny when we had frantically arrived at the emergency room and how during our stay they had burst into fall colors outside the hospital window. Now they lay on the ground in decay. I contemplated the cycle of life and wanted so much to deny the inevitability of it, but instead I focused on the bare branches of the trees, now strung with holiday lights in anticipation of the Christmas season. Something about the lights gave me a renewed sense of faith in the outcome. We had left on vacation the end of August and now we would be home just in time for Christmas. Although the prospects for Tino's health were fragile, as usual I would work on putting him back together again.

CHAPTER FIVE

THERE WOULD BE NINE more months of trying to nurse Tino back to health. I continued to take care of a massive wound that was left from the foot amputation, changed catheters, administered IV antibiotics, checked blood sugar levels, and sadly, pushed his wheelchair and otherwise did the best I could try to make his life as normal as possible. All of this care continued until the day I found myself staring down at Tino's lifeless body lying in the guesthouse.

A week of planning for Tino's funeral and waiting for family members to arrive went by before I finally found myself at the church he had chosen for the service. The church was filled to capacity and there were more people standing out in the parking lot. I sat in the front row with Tino's casket parked next to my left arm. I remember the cascade of orchids that covered the altar. The priest started the service by looking out across the sea of people and remarked that from the outpouring of attendance, it was obvious that Tino had made a huge impact on others.

Tino's wish was that he be cremated. He'd insisted that after his funeral we throw a lively party in celebration of his life. As I had always done throughout our life together, I planned a perfect event at our apartment building in San Salvador with his close family and friends. For music, I was sure to include Latin *boleros* and a few of his favorite Frank Sinatra tunes sprinkled in the playlist. Tino would have loved it. After presenting a slideshow of his life and our life together, I gathered all those who had come from the United States and returned to the lake house to continue the celebration. The next day I found myself standing in the living room full of friends and family waiting for Tino's ashes to arrive. Tino's sister entered the house holding a heavy wooden box that was still warm, a box as heavy as my heart. She handed it to me and then I went to the lake and started to walk down the many steps to the dock with Tino in my arms. The rest of the party followed behind me. I laid the box on the very boat seat where Tino had sat just seven days before, kicking back with a vodka tonic, telling funny stories to his best friend Bobby, and asking me to turn up the music so he could hear his favorite Latin love songs.

A lot can happen in a week, I thought.

I enjoyed a reflective moment with Tino's many grandchildren seated around me. In several pontoon boats filled with friends and family, we all cruised to an outcrop of rocks at the center of the lake. This was the perfect place for his ashes; the lake waters had run so deep within his soul.

I maneuvered the pontoon boat I was driving near one of the rocks that was peeking above the surface and turned off the motor. I then went to the front of the boat and knelt down to pour out the ashes. As the residual particles of Tino tumbled out of the box and into the water, my tears also fell into the lake and joined them. Everyone watched as all of who Tino had been washed into the sparkling waters of his beloved Lake Ilopango. We played his favorite mariachi song, "El Rey," which felt fitting and uplifting.

When we returned to the house, Tino's nephew Carlos insisted we get the party started again, just as Tino would have wanted. Everyone got into bathing suits, the drinks flowed, and we celebrated Tino "Tino style." It was almost four o'clock when we finally got out of the pool because storm clouds were approaching. As I headed for the dining table on the patio I happened to gaze out at the rocks where we had laid Tino's ashes just hours before. I paused, speechless. A brilliant rainbow arched across the lake, landing right on the rocks—a sign that all was as it should be. Tino's journey was complete.

After the funeral and all the festivities, the guests departed and I had to face our empty house alone. The silence was deafening. It is said that diabetes is the *silent killer*. Now the phrase took on a whole new meaning. The silence of the house became invasive, cutting into my soul. I could not imagine being there without Tino.

I seemed to be tethered to nothing except my lingering thoughts of Tino and how he died. That fatal moment would pass through my mind like a movie, frame by frame, and I would relive the experience over and over: fast forward, backward, slow, and consuming. I was being tortured by incessant thoughts about the moment he died. I had no way to escape, as my mind viciously injected ideas of failure into my soul. Tino is gone. Surely I could have done something more to save him.

Tino's leaving ruined me. I could not see a day in the future when I could ever smile or feel joyful again. Days turned into weeks. A month passed and nothing changed except for an ever-deepening sense of aloneness.

When my friend Linda invited me to spend a week with her at her beach house in Charleston, South Carolina, I was grateful for her reaching out to me. By the time I arrived in Charleston, a search for healing had begun, so Linda graciously took me to a bookstore where I headed right for the section on death and dying. There I sat, pulling book after book off the shelves. The terms *coping, grieving, loss, depression, healing,* and *starting over* mingled in my mind, making me realize that I had much work to do. The books gave me hope, but I smiled when I saw a "handbook," as if the solutions simply existed in a step-by-step approach!

My plan for coping with the adversity of being widowed was to educate myself. I was an incessant learner. As I gathered the books, I realized that I truly knew nothing about death, so I added *Grieving for Dummies* to my pile and headed for the cashier.

That night I got back to Linda's beach house with my new library of "dead books" and headed for the guest room. One book in particular stood out to me, which offered evidence drawn from research that life and love are eternal. This concept resonated with me. I was clinging to the hope that Tino had not really died and only his tortured body had undergone a physical death.

That night, after eating dinner with Linda, I stayed up and read touching stories of after-death communication and all sorts of fascinating things those on the "other side" had done to validate their existence for those they loved who were still here on "this side." I read how knowing these things brought peace to people like me who were in despair. The book validated my hope that love never dies.

I devoured the books I'd purchased over the next three nights, as my curiosity kept expanding into more and more questions about death and dying. In the process, I realized I had been so hell bent on keeping Tino alive that the concept of death had vanished from my consciousness. All my efforts had been about doctors, healing, and fixing. I had never accepted the idea of losing him.

As a lifetime overachiever and an entrepreneur with linear thinking used to crunching the numbers of success, I despised failing. Since I never had children, my maternal instincts instead were to breed success, bask in it, and personally gain from it, and then to spread the spoils to others so I could feel good about my efforts and myself. My goal since childhood was to have a successful career that would someday, by its nature, bring me a successful partner in marriage. After this ideal marriage was created, my interests were to have the perfect house, become the perfect hostess, be the perfect guest, and take perfect vacations—all necessary items on my checklist for the perfect world I was creating. By age fifty, the evolution of my ego was well developed and supported by Tino's ego. We were a perfectly matched pair.

Throughout my adult life, I felt that the only way to be complete was to ascribe to a model of acquisition that desired power and the feeling of being complete by owning more and receiving more and more possessions and accolades. I worked hard, usually twelve hours a day, and weekends were never off limits—especially when I was in the culinary world. All of this was done to hopefully experience a world of wealth and status, which I did until the day it all came crashing down around me as I held Tino's lifeless body in my arms. At that moment I came into the realization that I was holding the only thing in my life that truly mattered to me.

On the day that Tino died, all my ambitions, beliefs, successes, careers, and carefully crafted social roles dissolved. Suddenly and painfully, I was stripped of my identity and found I was truly alone.

After reading about death and near-death experiences and communication, I was fascinated by the possibility that the soul continued to exist in another realm. Did that mean it would be possible to talk to Tino? Until then, my experiences with "spiritual things" were mostly for entertainment's sake. Every now and then I would have a tarot card reading done for me, hire an expert in feng shui to energize my house, or bring in an animal communicator when my dogs didn't get along, but I did not have a deep understanding of spiritual matters.

After a few short days, I returned to El Salvador from South Carolina and lifted my heavy suitcase full of death books off the baggage belt. I left the airport and walked into the humidity that blanketed El Salvador after a summer of rain. Tino's driver Mario picked me up. Alonso and Reina who had met me on my first trip to El Salvador had resigned as they were miserable living in the city and left to live on a farm. I sat in the same passenger seat that a couple months before had held Tino as he was taking his last breaths. We made our way toward the rutted dirt road that would take me home.

For miles our vehicle struggled through the mud. Mario and I passed small huts and, like the hundreds of times that I had passed before, my compassion ran deep for those forced to carve out an existence in these homes with such limited resources. The spirit of the Salvadoran people always shined through when I saw their ingenuity for survival. It was my daily reminder of the necessity for gratitude in my own life, no matter how tragic things seemed at the moment.

The road continued to wind down the inner crevices of the dormant Ilopango volcano for another fifteen minutes of bumps and leaps through gushing roads and riverbeds swollen by the summer rains. Enormous leaves shaded us as we inched along the edges of the ridge, making our way to the lake nestled inside the crater. We ultimately arrived at the small village of Joya Grande, the community Tino and I had made our home for twenty years. Tino's family, the Novoas, had a special connection to the town. Most of the people who lived there had worked for Tino's father, who had owned and operated a large cattle ranch. Many of the older guys remembered roping cattle and riding horses with Tino when they were young. Their children also had fond memories of the Novoa children, who had all grown up there at the lake.

My car passed the school we had supported and the health clinic we had built. As always it was a joyful scene. Not much had changed there since the late 1800s, as there were still dirt roads and most people walked since they could not afford a car. Dogs darted in and out of cars and buses while pigs and cows happily roamed the streets. On the corner, a large woman was selling slices of watermelon and bags of cashews. Across the road from her, women balanced plastic jugs on their heads filled with water from the town's central well.

This was home, my piece of the world. Although it was surprising to many of my society friends in the capital, I cherished and loved living there. As we arrived at the peninsula where my house stood, I marveled at how the lush vegetation provided shelter for the bright orange chiltota birds that lived in the area. The neighborhood motmot birds with their exclamation point tails also darted in and out of the draperies of green, as if sharing in my excitement at returning home.

Finally, we reached the narrower part of the peninsula that extended far into the lake, where our house was. The gate swung open as our dogs, Bruno and Baco, greeted me, running behind the car until we reached the front door. I first saw my cook, Maria, come scurrying from the kitchen, drying her hands on an apron. When Maria smiled, everything smiled. Her dark skin and brown eyes made the perfect backdrop for her ivory teeth. Her long braid that bounced on her back was always in perfect order. Although she had little education, she was the smartest person I knew. Her intuition always guided her to understand everything she needed to know.

Carmen, who was in charge of cleaning and keeping the household organized, also approached. My heart sensed insecurity behind her happy grin. She was a light-skinned native woman with a robust figure that she managed well. Although still in despair, it was nice that there were these remarkable human beings happy to see me. I realized they were all that was left of the world that Tino and I had created together at the lake. I got out of the car near the spot that Tino had died and could still sense the air of grief in the driveway, as it seemed to linger in all our veins.

Maria wheeled my suitcase into the living room. She took out the books I was carrying and stacked them on the coffee table. I viewed them with a confidence that all my answers were just a few cups of coffee and a snuggle on the couch away.

CHAPTER SIX

OVER THE NEXT THREE months I continued to read tirelessly and engaged in a profound wondering about the intricacies of death. I was determined to discover the destination of Tino's soul, as well as to understand the journey it took, and in particular to explore the possibility that it remained intact.

Since my left hemisphere-dominant, logical brain was primarily in control throughout my lifetime, I felt that I needed tangible proof of the afterlife. I turned to researching scientific explanations of death with the same intensity I had when seeking treatments and cures for the complications related to Tino's diabetes. I was determined to find Tino's soul, wherever it was. I had to find the place where souls go.

Janet, a friend who was an animal communicator, called from Virginia to see how I was doing. Before we got off the phone, Janet told me that she sensed my deep desperation for answers about the afterlife and suggested that I get in contact with a world-class psychic medium, Deborah Harrigan, who was her good friend. I wrote down Deborah's phone number and placed it on top of the books on the coffee table.

I pondered the idea of connecting with Deborah, thinking she might be helpful in giving me some leads on Tino's current whereabouts, but also considering the religious view of seeking information through mediums.

I had struggled with my religious beliefs long before Tino's death. A lapsed Episcopalian, I had never connected emotionally with the concept of making confession to priests, like the Catholics do, or even to the social structure of worshipping in a church. Tino had been excommunicated from the Catholic Church due to his three divorces, so prior to our marriage he, too, had ended his affiliation with an organized religion. Although I did, and still do, embrace many of the teachings of Christ and the lessons of the Bible, I had always stumbled over the concepts of *heaven* and *hell*, as well as on the vagueness of teachings about the journey of the soul.

Living in El Salvador was like being a tea bag dipped into Catholic hot water. Everyone was supposed to be immersed in the Church's teachings. The politics of the country had the Church hovering on the sidelines of every issue. If you weren't on board, you stayed quiet about your alternative beliefs. This was surely a residual effect of how the Mayans must have felt after the Spanish arrived five centuries earlier when they were slaughtered for their beliefs. The lucky ones were those who did not die of imported diseases and were chosen to be sent to centers of conversion by missionaries.

Living on the outskirts of the capital of El Salvador, I always sensed the underlying current of the old ways, as pagan Mayan traditions still remained in use in many aspects of people's lives. These were practiced in spite of the threat of going to hell.

On a trip I took with Tino shortly after moving to Central America, we went to Chichicastenango, a Native village high in the hilltops of Guatemala. We entered the town square, which was very quiet, and walked into one of the two Catholic churches there. Inside we found a native shaman dancing around a statue of Christ that adorned the altar. We sat and watched the ritual with great curiosity. After several minutes, the shaman reached into his woven bag and pulled out two ears of corn and placed one in each of Christ's ears. Tino and I were on the verge of laughter as the shaman then left the church. We got up from our bench and, as we were leaving, found the local priest standing at the doorway. Tino asked him, "How long have you been trying to convert these people?"

The priest answered, "Four centuries."

In the aftermath of Tino's death, my focus was on reading my books, not on attending Sunday services. Since I was on a mission to find Tino's soul, which had taken a rather illustrious journey on Earth, I was pretty confident I would not find it in a church of any kind. Over the course of six months after I returned from Charleston, I read almost a hundred books about death written from every perspective imaginable. My voracious reading of this literature revealed an incredible spectrum of beliefs regarding the afterlife among all the world's religions and people. The consensus among most was that getting into heaven is the ultimate prize for those who stay connected to God throughout their lives. It is a reward for good behavior. When I reflected on that, I couldn't help thinking about the process Tino might be experiencing as he tried to get himself into heaven. It reminded me of the time he was on a long waiting list at Paradise Valley Country Club, one of the most exclusive or, shall I say, non-inclusive country clubs in Arizona, a bastion of waitlists and judgment.

Since Tino died suddenly and was not a dedicated churchgoer, after reflecting on the Christian view of gaining entrance to heaven I thought that perhaps we could have used a little more time readying ourselves for the application process. I smiled, pondering the scene that was possibly taking place of Tino's soul navigating through the process. Was it like going through customs in Honduras?

My moments of levity were brief. The truth is that I was desperate for a sign, for some sort of peek into the afterlife. Many sleepless nights I went outside and lay on the chaise longue under the stars with Bruno and Baco by my side and, in my deepest sadness, begged God and the universe to reveal Tino's whereabouts to me. I wanted some kind of acknowledgment that he was all right, intact, and still alive in some form of existence.

This was not the first time I had contemplated a deceased person's whereabouts. I had sat through many Catholic funerals in El Salvador that I felt were well-designed guilt trips for those in society to show up and be seen—with the added bonus that the more prominent the deceased, the fuller the collection plate. I admit that it crossed my mind whether some of the more morally compromised members of our society got a pass, or if there was work to do in some other "preheaven" place before they could get in. Perhaps there is a holding tank on the way to heaven where you work out the details of your "forgiveness of sins."

The tradition in El Salvador, as in most Latin American countries, is the option wherein families can have priests do additional masses known as *novenarios* to honor their loved ones for nine days, kind of like buying a supplemental insurance policy to assist the deceased by giving them an extra push to get to heaven.

Tino made it clear before he died that there was to be none of that for him. I guess he was confident that he could get in a priority boarding line at the gates of heaven on his own merits. After listening to the many sermons that often implied that only Catholics get a boarding pass to the flight to heaven, I often wondered whether people of other religions were put on standby or perhaps had a separate carrier. I finally concluded that Tino probably used his swagger and charisma to manage his way into heaven as he did in so many other important places, in spite of the fact that his earthly lifestyle might not have fit angelic rules.

I smiled while remembering a trip we made to Disneyworld. Tino decided to stay at the hotel and chill out while I went to the park with my nephews. We stopped back at the hotel to check on Tino and have lunch. When we got to the room, the television was on the ESPN channel, but Tino was gone. ESPN was covering an invitation-only event for the opening of the ESPN Club at Disney. We watched the program for a bit and then our mouths dropped open when we saw Mike Ditka and Magic Johnson standing with their arms around Tino and smiling at us on TV. When he got back to the hotel, I asked him how the hell he got into the party and he casually replied, "I saw the event on TV, and since it was here in Orlando, I decided to go. I grabbed a cab and just walked up the red carpet and told the hostess that I was Tino from El Salvador and she let me in."

Convincing myself he made the trip to the other side, I now needed to locate heaven and hell in the hope of finding him there or somewhere along the way. I looked for clues in a copy of the Bible that had been given to me by a family member, who, to this day, has great hopes for my reconversion to organized religion. I looked up *heaven* in the index and learned from the passage it led me to that it was supposed to be a real place with "streets paved in gold and other riches."

On the flip side was hell, a place where, if a person fails to choose the way of God (and for Christians, also Jesus), he remains for eternity, never to be resurrected bodily or spiritually. Either way, after reading these vague descriptions, I wanted more information about it than I found in the Bible.

I was feeling certain in my beliefs that God was not someone who would purposely judge us and cause us to suffer in hell. I believe that we come to Earth to make mistakes and learn from them, so to be punished for the real purpose we came here for seemed a total disconnect for me.

A pile of books later, and with the Bible still sitting on the coffee table, I was at the crossroads of understanding with my beliefs scattered like puzzle pieces. The time had come to put them together and establish my own definitions for concepts like *soul, transition, heaven, hell, resurrection, the other side,* and so on. The most elusive piece of the puzzle was death itself and the fear of it, which I would later learn was the greatest obstacle to my future enlightenment. I was in the process of realizing that religion, as I was taught to practice it, was also an obstacle to the truth; there were too many barriers and rules obscuring the answers I was seeking. My thirst for knowledge was deeper than the filters of a religious context.

Life was also trying to move me back into normalcy. On weekends, in keeping with Tino's tradition, I would sit in the same corner of the pool where we had spent countless afternoons, he with a cold beverage in his hand. I could still hear the laughter there and recalled how his one-liners kept people in the pool well into the evening—by default the food would then be served poolside. Tino treated his impending death with the same levity he had so much of his life. On several occasions, even with the pool full of friends, a kettle of vultures would fly overhead, diving through the afternoon winds. Tino would look up at them and say, "Not yet, you sons of bitches!"

While living in such a remote place, I was fortunate to have the internet so I could manage our business and personal matters from the lake. After Tino died, mornings were spent trying to assimilate my responsibilities for all our pending projects in my own style. Afternoons involved more reading and more downloads onto my Kindle reader. Over the months, my collection of books was becoming more and more about spirituality, and much less about religion. Facing the prospect of either heaven or hell was the basis of almost all religious fears and I'd had enough of fear, living several years in wartorn El Salvador and now alone in a jungle. It was clear to me that when I scrapped most religious theories I could come to better terms with death. If I could just break through my limiting beliefs, I could expose my soul, which would take the stage and begin the journey to find Tino.

I wanted a deeper sense of who God really was. In the past I had thought of God as a being who existed apart from the world, controlling it from somewhere else in the universe. As a child, I thought he lived next door to Santa Claus.

My other reality was that I had no "go to" friends, no social safety net, because much of my time had been invested in caring for Tino. My priority was keeping our lives and responsibilities intact, so I was isolated and without external support. I wept for days upon days, hours upon hours—in the boat, under the tree in the driveway where Tino died, and in his office as I sorted through every shred of paper, hoping for a secret message or to discover a link to where he was. Darkness would fall at night, and my heart yearned for Tino even more. Morning would come and I would reach across the bed, as I always had, to hug him and give him a kiss, but my hand landed on an empty pillow. By now my three beautiful Persian cats, Footsie, Toe, and Canela, had divided up the space where Tino had always been. They must have sensed that a deep depression was overtaking me and wanted to be close enough for me to feel comforted.

To make matters worse, I would press the start button in iTunes for Latin Love Songs, which was a constant punishment. I was alone with eighty acres of land between me and my nearest neighbor, and when I couldn't sleep I would go outside and wish for answers to fall like the many stars I saw racing across the moonless skies. I reflected continually on all the choices I had made in my life that caused me to end up in this place alone.

Lake Ilopango is a deep lake, born out of the greatest explosion in the western hemisphere in 536 c.e. This eruption likely spread ashes around the world. It is a place where nature has existed in its present form for thousands of years, and it has survived the degradation of the environment that is caused by human civilization because it is so isolated. With wild cats, iguanas, snakes, armadillos, foxes, and a symphony of birds, it is an extraordinary place to live. Most of the Mayans who lived there in ancient times had to make a fast exit and thousands and thousands of them perished, unable to escape the explosion that was so massive that it spread ashes and darkness across the Northern Hemisphere—even as far as Europe and Asia. Scientists have now determined this led to catastrophic crop failures and climate change, leading to famines and disease that killed millions and began the Dark Ages.

One of my frequent walks was to the highest point of the peninsula, where I could see the water on both sides. When Tino was still alive, I often went there to disconnect from caring for him and take some time with just the dogs and me. As I stood up on the point one afternoon, the scene shifted and I blinked several times, trying to get back to "normal." Suddenly I felt my cells blend into the cells of everything that was there; this was a whole new take on being one with nature.

I remembered returning to the house that day and telling Tino about the remarkable thing had just happened to me. He looked at me quizzically, and then his crooked smile appeared, the one that celebrated the touch of craziness in me that kept his life whimsically unpredictable.

Since that experience at the top of the peninsula, I had always seen myself as a pile of cells in the form of a body, so it later made sense when I read that every cell in the human body rejuvenates itself at least once every seven years. Our bodies completely change, yet with all that, we maintain the essence of who we are.

So then, what remains when we die?

I settled on the understanding that what remain when the body dies and decays are the soul and the mind. In looking for the spirit of Tino, I was left with no other option than to trash the notion that what exists is only what can be seen or measured. I concluded that the soul and the mind are a ball of consciousness that transcends the life experience. This is the truth of who we really are.

I continued to spend hours sorting out new concepts I was discovering. After defining these to my simple satisfaction, I knew my next focus would be to go further than my current beliefs to find Tino's soul. I felt compelled to determine what had become of it when he transitioned from his body into his spiritual form. I was sure his soul was something that was able to separate from the body, as I had felt something literally leaving Tino at the moment of his death. I also believed in eternal life for every living thing.

I became convinced that there was another reality, one apart and distinct from what we see with our eyes, so I stopped limiting myself to the concept seeing is believing.

Over the initial months following Tino's death, when I was grieving my loss, I felt that my true healing from Tino's transition would be found in knowing with certainty that the soul transitions from the body to another place which the books I was reading called *the other side,* and that the other side is not a destination where there is fear and judgment. It is instead a place where the soul resides, and where the essence of any individual we have ever known survives.

CHAPTER SEVEN

I T WAS NOW THREE months after Tino's death. I held the small paper in my hand with the psychic medium Deborah Harrigan's phone number on it. I began to dial her number and my finger trembled over each button I pushed.

Deborah, who had a bubbly and effervescent personality, was immediately welcoming. Before we would form any connection to Tino, she insisted that I knew the basics of spiritual communication. Deborah took two hours to explain these to me. She shared that spirits or transitioned loved ones express themselves best through impressions and feelings; because she was more sensitive to these impressions than the rest of us it was her job to put those into words that precisely reflected the meaning and the intent of the spirit on the other side.

Deborah explained that at times the actual words from those on the other side are spoken through her. However, spirits often show her a vision of what they want to express, which for them can be an easier way to communicate with us. A picture tells a thousand words, after all. Deborah emphasized that making the right connection to our loved ones is not a matter of picking up a phone and calling them. It was her job to attune to the same vibrational channel as the deceased. She did this by questioning the deceased to elicit verifying details. What was remarkable to her was that the spirit of a deceased person would come through to her with the same personality.

There were no guarantees that a spiritual connection would be made on any occasion. Success, Deborah informed me, relies entirely on the willingness of the person who has transitioned to enter into a communication with those who are still here. Whether or not they connect is entirely up to their discretion, but Deborah's experience had shown her that they were almost always enthusiastic to connect.

Since Tino's death was so sudden, a lot had been left unsaid when he transitioned. Deborah shared that speaking with him could be an opportunity to address any misperceptions so that we would have full closure and ensure a positive outcome for both of us in our future spiritual growth.

Deborah went on to explain that she typically works with a group of spirit guides and teachers who are standing by in another spiritual dimension as the communication takes place. We all have spiritual guides like these. Hers were there to ensure that the integrity of the message comes through and that her client will receive it in a way that it was intended. Often her guides would correct or expand on an expression used by Deborah if they sensed that the client was misunderstanding the intent.

Working as a psychic, like Deborah did, is both a simple and a complex process for the psychic. In Deborah's case sometimes communicating a message just boiled down to offering a word-to-word expression of it or using a combination of the two processes of describing a visual image and saying the words she heard in her head. Deborah told me that she had no idea of the importance of certain words to me, since Tino and I would have the only true knowledge of our relationship. A medium should be simply a channel for information to flow through; there should not be any attachment to the message.

It excited me to know that the words would come through to me "untouched" and therefore authentic to his character, which would help me in believing it was really him. I was hungry to connect to some aspect of Tino again.

As Deborah established the landscape for communicating, I was excited to think that during the session she could bridge the distance between me and Tino. She would now be his voice. Her explanation was kind and gentle and was an acknowledgment that it was possible to communicate with those who have transitioned. Deborah's grandmother and mother both had the gift of psychic knowledge and had passed it on to Deborah, who I knew from Janet was an exceptional psychic. Being with someone as gifted as Deborah, I knew I was in a secure place and that I had the right person steering the wheel into this uncharted territory.

As our time together was coming to an end, Deborah's voice suddenly shifted, because Tino had come into our session. She said, "Lori, it was not a stroke. It was a heart attack first, and then a blood clot went into the brain and he was gone."

I was silent and moved. I had not yet shared the specifics of Tino's death with Deborah, but she had described it perfectly. Still stunned at the accuracy of her statement, I made an appointment with her to connect me to Tino again the very next day.

★ ★ ★

The next morning, with great anticipation, I sat at Tino's desk with a stack of blank paper in front of me, ready to take notes during our first "date" since he had left. Nervously, again I called Deborah on the phone and she explained that all our sessions would be held in a sacred space, so before we got going she called in her spirit guides and others with whom she worked from the spirit world. Then she invited Tino to come into the space she had created. Deborah started by saying that he was there in her office and described him perfectly to me when he was the age of fifty-five, and not as he appeared when he was sick and dying. He was young, vibrant, and full of energy. I would later learn that he was very proud of pulling this off, as he was able to morph into the image of his prediabetic human body.

I sensed from Deborah that she was a little skeptical of Tino's comfort level in her office, but she let it slide this time since she was taken by him. She had no idea of the depth of the personality she was about to meet, since I had shared nothing about him with her except his photograph. She seemed a little agitated that he had put his feet on her desk and presented himself smoking a cigarette. Even though the smoke was etheric, of course, Deborah asked him to stub out the cigarette and return his feet to the floor.

Even though Tino quit smoking shortly after we were married, I grinned at the scene as she described it. It was very Tino, always wanting to be the center of attention, but he had also met his match in Deborah. She was the kind of person who was capable of putting him in his place and setting the rules for his spiritual chats with me.

The conversation started with Deborah saying, "Lori, take notes. Tino has a list of things he would like you to do since he left. He says to call the lawyer because he is dragging his feet with the inheritance issues. Check the mileage of the motor in the boat; it is probably due for an oil change. Watch the staff, as they are being lax since he left. Check on the accountant, as he is lazy. And the driver was not honest with you about where he was going many times."

In total disbelief, I took diligent notes and made the list as instructed. At the same time, it felt strange to be in such a natural conversation as if nothing had transpired between us. I guess I had expected him to say hi and ask, "Lori, how are you doing on Earth since I left?" What was reassuring to me was that he seemed to have a sense of what was going on. It validated that he was around.

After further reflection, I knew that if there had been anything that would have driven Tino crazy, it was leaving the way he did and not being able to give me a list of things to do. Again, very Tino-like. The whole scene was seamless, as if he was really just on the other end of the phone.

Deborah described the sensation of Tino arriving in her space as "swooping in." Later, for me this would become his energetic trademark. Although Tino was uncertain and confused that day and had many questions as to where he was and how things "worked," as he described it, he seemed like he was near, because he was trying to run things.

My own expectations, derived from a lot of what I had read, were that he would be describing some angelic place with white columns where he was hanging out with his deceased relatives—but instead, *I get a to-do list?* I took my notes and, since we were on the topic of things to do, I thought I would get some of my own pending issues out of the way while I had Tino "on the line."

I had been looking for his gun permits for months without success. He told me they were in the glove compartment of his car, where I found them immediately after our session. After the call I also consulted with Edgardo, the caretaker of our property and husband of my cook, Maria, and verified that, yes, Tino had reminded him about the maintenance on the boat right before he died. He promised that he would get right on it, as he had forgotten. It was also true that the lawyer was taking longer than Tino would have wanted on the estate and inheritance issues.

With the to-do list out of the way, we moved on to Tino's explanation of what occurred the day he died. He died of two blockages in his brain. The first one affected his ability to speak and the second took his life force. Tino was very focused on how it felt when he died and wanted me to know every last physical detail about it. After sharing all these details, he was happy to report that he had regained his health and mobility. He was strong and very much alive. No longer would he be burdened with the complications of diabetes that had caused him to have both feet partially amputated. He was especially pleased that he could do everything for himself now.

Then he moved on to my role as a caregiver. He shared how grateful he had felt for the twenty-four hours a day I spent caring for him and regretted that he had kept his gratitude to himself. As he said this, a surge of deep compassion came through me. Tino said that now, from his new perspective where he could see life more clearly, he understood the importance of gratitude. He realized he had taken many things for granted.

Tino shared that when I was in a dream state he found it easy to connect with me, and if I was more cognizant of those times when he was entering into my consciousness I would be able to realize that he was often the source of my thoughts.

He told me emphatically that the spirits where he was were not there because of their religious beliefs, but by natural law. Going to church was not a prerequisite for going to heaven (which I am sure was of great relief to him). He also said it was not right for priests to have a monopoly on defining existence.

Eventually the subject changed to our pets, and Tino told me that he was so happy to have seen all of our deceased pets around him when he passed. It made me happy to know he was surrounded by unconditional love.

Tino was in a state of change and I was reminded by him that he had no needs. He emphasized how awkward it felt that he could no longer truly worry about things. "It just doesn't work here," he shared. "My earthly emotions were different than my emotions are here." Deborah told me he was showing her that he was "trying" to feel frustrated because he was unable to tell me what to do. Hearing this, I pictured his ghostlike figure following me around, unable to get my attention.

Tino described his "frustration" and other emotions as concepts, something that he had a memory of, yet without a body he was incapable of truly feeling frustrated. Since he was still in a process of healing and not completely grounded, he was longing to feel bonded with the Earth, even though he was actually in a state of contentment. He admitted that he still had a great love for food and wine and that the smell of a good wine still lingered with him. He said that he often popped into the kitchen to see what Maria was preparing me for dinner, but joked that he rarely found me there—implying that he had seen my total loss of interest in cooking.

Tino told me he was not prepared for what happened. His transition was as big a surprise to him as it was to me. He was therefore still struggling to understand where he was and the form in which he existed. I realized this was a complicated process since he still had the point of view of an earth being who needed material proof for everything he saw and experienced. I knew with him being a left-brained civil engineer with a logical mind that he was probably struggling to explain his current existence.

He said he was like a child, learning through his new experiences on the other side. Much like me, he was questioning all the beliefs he had accumulated over the years.

Deborah, who knew nothing about Tino's personality, commented, "Lori, he has such a huge presence. When he walked into my room he dominated the space. Thank goodness I am sure of myself, as he could have been intimidating. He has a confidence that what he says is always relevant."

Tino then chimed in and said, "Of course I am always right!"

This got a big laugh from the three of us.

During the session, Deborah's voice changed frequently. She explained, "Tino is using my voice box and sometimes the vibration of the messages changes speed as he tries to adapt to my voice. Tino seems surprised that his voice does not sound like his own since he is speaking through me."

The energy lightened a little and he was very quick to make a comment about the medical profession. "They are not right 100 percent of the time," he said, "for if they were, I would not be on the other side talking to you. I would instead be planning our next party and having a drink."

One bone of contention for Deborah and Tino in the session was his use of inappropriate words for getting his point across. Deborah refused to use his "colorful vocabulary." At one point, Tino flew off with naughty words in English and Spanish, and I heard Deborah say, "Nope. I am not going there." I then heard a one-sided argument about Tino's choice of words until they came to some sort of understanding and the session continued.

Tino was very excitable at times in life, and apparently also in death. When I asked a tough question, she said he was pacing back and forth in her office while he contemplated his answer with his hands on his hips. As usual, when he was speaking he would make broad gestures with his arms. Deborah scolded him to "calm down and not be so stressed out." She described him perfectly as he was when he was alive.

Deborah finally asked me if I wanted to say anything more to Tino before the session closed. I sat in silence, overwhelmed by fact that I was really talking to Tino. In a slow and quiet voice, I said, "You're still you."

Tino replied, "Yes, Lori, who else would I be?"

CHAPTER EIGHT

B Y THE END OF our first session, I was filled with gratitude for Deborah and her abilities, and for the extraordinary opportunity to connect with Tino. We made plans to
talk again so I could continue my conversation.

I walked out on the patio and sat down with the dogs.
My mind raced back to romantic times with Tino as I tried
to resurrect the sensation of having his arms around me. He
cared deeply for me and was always concerned about my
safety. Who would be calling on the phone to see if I was
okay now?

I was remembering the first time he ever touched me.
We were in his car and he put his hand on top of my hand
and kept it there for the drive home. It was a simple gesture,
but energy surged through me as I realized that there was a
connection between us that was so much deeper than I had
ever felt with anyone.

I also loved dancing with Tino, hanging my arms
around his neck and looking into his eyes where I would find
the depths of his smile. I thought back to him teaching me
to dance from the waist down not flinging my arms around

"like a *gringa*," as he would say. It didn't take me long for my legs to find the rhythm so that our bodies were perfectly intertwined.

I looked out over the lake, remembering so many moons that had splattered light across the water while Tino and I were dancing to Latin love songs until late in the evening when he would grab my hand and head us toward the bedroom. I cannot think of another place in the world that compared to being on the edge of Lake Ilopango with Tino. The backdrop of where we lived and being with Tino had been a lingering honeymoon that I thought would never end.

A month passed after my first session with Deborah, and I had new questions prepared. I called Deborah very excited to hear and feel Tino again.

Tino was a very well-known person in El Salvador's society, therefore his death had not gone unnoticed. He had hundreds of friends and associates and was a founder of many of El Salvador's important institutions. He had been in politics and had a national presence. Even though his influence had waned in recent years, many fondly recalled his dynamic approach to things. The newspaper had published a full-page obituary when he died, emphasizing his wit and humor as something that defined him.

Tino had been very clear that he wanted a party celebrating his life after the funeral, which was rather unconventional for Salvadoran society. I was eager to talk with him about it, as I felt I had pulled it off with a lot of novelty for those who had attended. I'd been determined to grant his wishes despite efforts by some family members to put their own religious spin on it and I was very proud about how I handled it and was curious to hear his view on the entire day.

"So what did you think about the funeral?" I asked.

"I was suddenly there, as if I just appeared," Tino answered. "At first for me it seemed like another social function. I was not really aware that it was a funeral, especially mine. I was walking among the guests—it was not a physical walking, but a movement. I could sense sorrow around me. I was feeling sorry for all the sadness."

While describing the funeral, Tino took Deborah and me back to the scene in the mortuary where his body lay before being wheeled to the nearby church for the service. He described not being in the coffin at all. To the contrary, he was mingling around the room taking account of who was there and who was not. He said he even checked out the names in the book that I had left out for people to sign. He saw me moving around, but as we had done at most parties, he was making the rounds with his own agenda.

"I did not want to be too near the energy of my family," Tino said, "as their hearts were very steeped in grief—especially yours, Lori—and it was difficult to see the pain in everyone I cared about.

"I was also very confused. I felt like I had a body, but there was none. I wanted to hug people and console them, but I realized I had no arms.

Of course, I now understand that when I was there I was dead, but when it happened I did not see it that way. I felt like a person who was at the funeral of another person, as my thoughts had not accepted that it was actually my funeral.

"I was surprised when I saw that you were the grieving widow and not someone else. My casket was right next to you, and I kept telling you to stop focusing on the casket, as I was not in it. But you were too caught up in the grief of my leaving, and I could not reach you. At the church, I stayed near the altar and watched and listened from there.

"When I realized that no one could see me, I decided to have some fun with it. I meandered between the pews and focused especially on those who were whispering or talking, even though I could also understand their thoughts. Oh, that was fun! People wanting to know how much money I had, what was in my will, and what you would do now. There were others talking about where they were going for lunch and gossiping.

"I saw my old golf buddies and wondered what you would do with my golf cart. But every time I eavesdropped on conversations between people my spirit eyes would always end up on you, Lori. The painful energy coming from your heart concerned me because I did not know what would now become of you.

"I could not speak, but I could hear everyone. And although I did not have my body as a foundation for my own emotions, the memory of the emotions lingered and I felt sadness, especially for you. I knew my children would all go back to Arizona after the funeral. My immediate family in El Salvador, whose members struggled to embrace my free spirit and lack of religious faith, would abandon you.

"My body was wheeled out of the church and into the hearse, to be driven off for cremation. That is when I realized my body was not going to be around anymore. Did it bother me? No, I did not have a feeling either way. I guess I looked with nostalgia for the old body that used to sustain my shitty golf swing, but any attachment was only to the memories of the limitations it had. I was most interested in the after-mass party, so I left the church and waited for everyone at our apartment in town. I went to check the bar to be sure everything was in order, and I wanted to be sure you had not overlooked anything for my 'exit party.'

"I was pleased that everyone was together, but I wanted very much to be seen. It bothered me a lot that no one could see me. When I would pop out to the lake house, the dogs and cats could sense my presence, but the people could not see me. At times I would just sit down at a table waving my hands in front of their faces, but nothing. For me, a person who always wanted to be the center of attention and the life of the party, this took some getting used to. I watched as you spread my ashes on the lake and loved that you played 'El Rey' in my honor. That put a smile on my face. Good choice, sweetie.

"During the lively after-funeral party, I could see two of the guides who had brought me to the funeral standing near the corner. Eventually they telepathically said that it was time for me to leave, so I left with them. There was much work to do to overcome the sensation of separation from everyone, especially for me who was always 'on' in those situations. It was also a stretch to realize that I did not have a glass of Johnny Walker on the rocks in my hand, so I was taken by my guides to a 'decomposing place' —no pun intended—where I would be able to process the newness of my transitory state."

When Tino finished describing his funeral there was silence from Deborah. I guessed that for her to go back in time to capture Tino's impressions she would have to be deep in trance so I waited a while. Then I asked, "Deborah, did you catch any of that?"

She replied, "No Lori. I wasn't there when Tino was describing things through me to you."

I began to tell her what Tino had said and we just cracked up thinking of him snooping around at his funeral, eavesdropping on all the conversations. It brought a laugh from Tino, too, who felt he had described it well.

I told Deborah, "I would like Tino to describe to me what it was like when he died. What was his perception of those around him when it happened?"

Deborah immediately broke into hysterics and could hardly get the answer to me as he jokingly started his response. "What is she asking? What the hell is she asking that question for?"

"Here I am, dying, and she wants know what she looked like? I am in the process of dying, and you are asking me what I saw? God damn it, Lori, I was in the process of dying! I was busy at that moment. Believe me, I was not paying attention to what everyone looked like!

"Okay, so I was transitioning and, yes, I was cognizant of all the people around me. One minute I was there with you, and the next minute I was gone—but now, today, you want a damned detailed report on what it looked like?"

Deborah and I were both on the floor, almost speechless with laughter. I knew I was not going to get a straight answer because Tino was in one of his funny moods.

Before I hung up, however, Deborah said, "Wait, Lori. He is getting serious now. His energy is coming into a different view of that time."

The conversation stilled for a moment. Then Tino, in deep reflection, focused on the moment of his death as he said slowly, "Okay, so I died. That thought is a revelation since I do not think of myself as dead—or that I do not exist or that there is nothing to me. So when you speak of dead people the words get crossed, as the earthly meaning of *dead* does not accurately reflect the state I am in. I realize now that it was death itself at that moment, but what does that mean? The word *dead* does not define me.

"Those on Earth see death as a void, believing that we are gone. But here, on the other side, it is different for us, since we are not gone. I can still feel your presence and see you. I am not as blind and limited as you are."

Tino then went on to describe his desire at times to influence things. "It was a realization that my energy would have little impact on things, because from where I am the effect is much less forceful than when I was on Earth. At different times, if I am pushy enough with my vibration, I can get you to notice or do something. I keep chiseling away relentlessly until you finally hear me. I know you will eventually hear me, but in a different way. When I see you are going to do something I do not agree with, I want to burst in and tell you. I will say, though, that you have handled things well, even with all you've had to deal with."

As usual, Tino was in rare form. I asked him if there was anything he needed from me and he said yes. "Next time you go out to the rocks where you put my ashes, bring me a Johnny Walker, my favorite cheese, and a tortilla."

With the conversation over, I hung up the phone with a dull ache. I had to say goodbye again. I was overwhelmed as there was so much to sort out about what I had heard and felt. The call forced me into a realm of multiple possibilities. I had just had a very convincing and surprisingly normal experience talking with my—for lack of a better term—*dead husband*. It was remarkably seamless in its content and delivery although my husband's words were being delivered by a woman I'd never met face to face.

What kept going through my mind was that Tino was very much alive. My rational mind was racing as its interpretations of death were being rattled. Tino was perfectly intact with his pure essence and personality as vibrant and loving as before he left. He was just somewhere else, in a place I could not entirely imagine.

I did not have another conversation with Tino right away, as I wanted to reflect on whether these interactions would be helpful to him on the other side and to me, the human being remaining behind here on Earth. It was also time to try and create a normal life and do my best to manage things in El Salvador. I had always been resourceful and had a natural talent for business. I had really been the one running things for the last five years of our marriage. Having to attend to issues that required my attention was what kept me moving forward. Tino and I had so many plans, yet now my enthusiasm for them was at rock bottom. It seemed so useless to consider doing anything alone.

I tried to be more supportive of the people who were working for me. I would go into the office once in a while and try to be relevant, but the spark was gone. Problems resulted from my lack of interest, so time was spent putting out fires that occurred because of my indifference.

In late November, a huge storm dumped three feet of rain in less than eight hours, almost wiping out Joya Grande. There were also precarious landslides occurring around the house. I was completely isolated for two months, having to navigate by boat to get out of the lake area, as all the roads were washed out. I mounted a massive rescue effort in Joya Grande, which was very isolated.

One morning, as I was standing in the makeshift distribution center I had set up in a simple church, an old woman with a carved leather face approached me and asked, "Doña Lori, I lost my house, all my possessions, and my grandson, what do I do?" I felt her pain just as it were mine. I wrapped my arms around her and we cried.

Finally I put my hands on her shoulders and said, "Have faith. All who have lost those we love will find a way to peace somehow."

Because of the penetrating eyes of that woman and the depth of her loss, I realized that my loss did not give me a monopoly on sadness and that I should do more about being aware of helping others than licking my own wounds.

For over a week I shuttled food and supplies in my pontoon boat. The U.S. Embassy called and had me receive helicopters on the beach filled with necessities. I must have called the Minister of Public Works fifty times begging for tractors that finally opened the road. With hundreds of people standing outside my makeshift office at the relief center, I would ask for miracles to come. And they came—every single day—in pickup trucks, boats, and helicopters with food and necessities for the town's survival. At night I would worry about how I was going to feed everyone, and the next day there was always enough to go around.

Little did I realize that the spirit world had immersed me in the tragic loss of many so that by helping others I could begin to help myself.

CHAPTER NINE

IT WAS NOW THE Christmas season. Clean up and support in the town was almost over. My job of helping people get on with their lives kept me greatly satisfied. A Mennonite group arrived and started building new houses for those who had lost theirs. I felt my time there was nearing completion. I took my fake Christmas tree to the center of town and strung some lights on it, feeling that I had done all that I could for the time being.

The heaviness of the first Christmas without Tino weighed heavily on me. My plans would take me to Scottsdale to be with Tino's children, to the place where the whole chapter of my life with Tino had begun. But going back to Arizona was difficult for me. The plane ride was excruciating as I had an empty seat beside me, a cutting reminder that Tino was absent. After arriving at the Phoenix airport, I sat in the garage of the rental car center crying and not wanting to come to terms with the end of a relationship that began twenty-three years before. Our story had come full circle, our time together on Earth had ended. It seemed so final, as if a sharp knife had separated us. My soul did not know how to tell me that it was time to close the chapter.

I managed to get through the days before Christmas by focusing on the preparations and looking forward to being with family.

I had been struggling with the ultimate decision of distributing some of Tino's personal treasures to others in the most meaningful way. Tino had a beautiful gold watch, and I was trying to find the best way to pass on its value to his daughters and stepson. I had taken it to different stores to see what options there were for trading it in and finding the perfect gift for each of them. Every time I walked into a jewelry store, however, I burst into tears at the thought of selling it. I would then put it back in my pocket and leave. This happened several times, always with the same results.

Even for this watch, time was literally running out. It was two days before Christmas without Tino, and I still had his timepiece in my pocket. I decided to try again; I went to a shop at a mall where the salesperson agreed that the watch was valuable. After consideration, however, he suggested I go to another jewelry shop as his did not work with trade-ins.

I left, at a leisurely stroll, window-shopping until that same swooping energy I felt during the most recent session with Deborah came in and started pushing me. A voice in my head was also telling me to get going to that other store! I ignored it at first, but the pushing sensation continued, until I finally felt I had no other choice than to pick up the pace and get back to my car. Even as I was thinking of stopping at another place along the way, the voice came through again, with a bit more urgency. "No stopping! Go straight to the store!"

This energy was very much like Tino. It was so familiar to me, as once he made a decision he was always full speed ahead on it. I began to sense I had been put on a mission, so there was no time to waste.

I arrived at the jewelry store and sat in the back room with a gold trader as he evaluated the watch, and we reached a final price. He then escorted me out to the showroom to take a look around. I had no idea what I would buy, but I did feel sure I was in the right place to find something special. I was immediately drawn to the center case of jewelry. There were several lovely crosses, and next to the collection was the name Konstantino. Tino's full name was the same except with a "C" for Constantino. Almost in disbelief at the perfect connection, I chose the pendants, one for each daughter. It was an emotional moment when I shared the story and gave the girls their necklaces.

This was the first time that I "heard" Tino without the message coming through Deborah. At the time I could not validate that he was speaking to me, but the energy felt so "him" that I made that assumption. I marveled at the possibility that Tino and I could actually communicate, each from where we were.

I do not know how I survived the holidays with my heart so empty. The day after Christmas I got in the car and drove by the house where we had spent our first Christmas together and parked in front of it as the memories came swirling out of the front door. I remembered the waving Santa and smiled.

Then it was New Year's Eve, an event I was dreading. When the clock struck midnight, I felt like Cinderella looking around for a prince. Instead, the grandkids had the big-screen TV playing music videos as they danced, singing and gyrating, to Beyoncé. I fought the irony as she sang "All the

Single Ladies." I did my best to add to the festive moment by flinging one of the hot pink feather boas around my neck and putting on a cheesy tiara with "Happy 2010" on it.

Inside, all I wanted to do was slap on a sticky note reading "Unhappy 2010."

It was finally New Year's Day and I was relieved that I had made it through the holidays. Confetti and feathers from the boas were scattered in all corners of the house. Everyone else had gone home. Looking out the upstairs window at Camelback Mountain, memories rushed in, as it was the same view I would wake up to in bed with Tino when we first started living together. I wanted desperately to talk to him again so I picked up the phone and called Deborah. It was time to check in.

With Deborah's help, I asked Tino to reflect on the holidays and he described our gathering this way: "I loved watching all of you dancing with the feather boas around your necks." I was awestruck to have him mention the boas; this was another huge validation that I was really talking to Tino—that he was truly around.

He then said, "It was like seeing you all for the first time with different eyes. What I had with my family I did not know, nor realize its importance. I was a man with great pride and little humility while I was on Earth."

Tino's attention then turned to his gold watch. He was very pleased that I had gotten the message.

After this session I realized that even though Tino was still Tino, death was changing him. The ego and his past view of things—always wanting things to be right or wrong—were dissolving as he was realizing that his perceptions of others were no longer critical. I felt him softening into assuming the place of a bystander and not being the center of attention as he was throughout his life. He seemed now to take a spiritual view of things, understanding that we are all connected and no one is less or more than another. The roles that he had played in his life—of father, son, husband, and friend—had ended and the force of his energy in our lives was dissipating.

With the holidays over, I returned to El Salvador. It was now the dry season and they were taking the Christmas decorations down at the airport as I moved through customs to see Mario, our driver, waiting. On the way home from the airport, we passed the trucks full of just-picked coffee and flatbeds piled to the brim with stalks of sugarcane. Life was going on everywhere around me, yet, I was stuck. I was becoming ever more detached and retreating further and further inside myself.

Months went by and I was still bathed in grief. I could not bring myself out of the feeling of desperation I had in trying to save Tino and failing. There were so many days I could not get out of bed, and I began to recognize the symptoms of a major depression. I rarely left my house or went outside. I could not generate enough positive thoughts to shift myself out of this deep despair. Maria and Carmen were worried, knocking on my bedroom door as I sat in isolation. I would respond positively so I could buy a few more hours before they came to check again. I was merely going through the motions of life. This was indeed the blackest hole I had ever been in.

I contacted Deborah again and told her I needed help. As usual, she offered her generous words of comfort and understanding. We agreed that it would be a good time to talk to Tino again. It was now March and during the session he recognized all of the emotions I had been feeling over several months.

He described it this way: "You do not sleep well." He then showed Deborah and me an image of the color green and told me, "Geez, Lori, go outside in nature. You are stuck in a tomb that you have made for yourself. You need to go outside to heal. Take a retreat and look for renewal for your body, mind, and spirit. You need to leave the tomb you are in so you are able to breathe again. I died, but I am alive! Lori, it is you who are dead!"

I knew he was right, but struggled nonetheless to put back together the pieces of my broken heart. It felt impossible. Even though my continuing conversations with Tino felt so real, I would spiral into doubt and often questioned if it truly was Tino whom I was contacting through Deborah. I needed more. I wanted something I could touch and feel— not just some hope that I really was speaking with the man I had loved so exquisitely for so long.

Another Sunday had arrived and I realized that I needed to get out of the house or else I would drown in sorrow. I had Edgardo help me get the boat out, then I put Bruno and Baco on board and headed out on the lake.

Lake Ilopango is a large body of water and without Tino in the boat I felt very small, but I pushed on. I saw that Maria had packed a cooler and when I opened it I found she had prepared it precisely to Tino's specifications. Beer, wine, vodka, and mixers were inside, all ready for the party that might happen. I smiled at her consistency, yet my heart knew the party was over.

I turned the boat toward the center of the lake and headed to los cerros quemados ("the burnt rocks") that were the core of the volcano and where Tino's ashes had been placed. As I drew near, I lowered the speed and quietly approached, thinking about the rainbow again. I kept trying to convince myself it could not possibly be a coincidence—that it was truly a gift for me. It was a restless time of grief. I was going through an angry stage, feeling mad at God for taking Tino and causing my world to come crashing down. I wanted proof that he and so much more existed beyond my reality.

Standing on the edge of the boat, I screamed, "I want a sign!" The sound echoed across the lake and bounced off the volcano walls.

I was waiting for a response when, all of a sudden, a very large duck with a white belly came swooping around the boat and then landed on the rocks. Startled, I continued to watch while this duck made himself very comfortable on the outcropping.

I started up the engine and went nearer for a better look. There were other ducks of different species on the rocks that day, and all flew away when I started to get closer except the one that flew over the boat when I called. He did not move an inch. I also noticed he had taken up permanent residence. I stayed and we sat staring at each other. I asked him, "So what do you know about the guy whose ashes are here and how do you manage being out in the middle of Lake Ilopango all alone?" I was hoping for some duckly advice.

Time passed. Intrigued by the duck, I would go every Sunday to see if he was still there, and he was. We would "talk" about death and how it changes everything, and about a lot of other pressing issues that you would talk to a duck about. A friend of mine did some research on the duck and identified it as a *Sula leucogaste* or brown booby. After fifteen years of living on the lake, I had never seen a duck like this one before. More remarkable to me was the fact that this particular species of duck always lives in pairs and in large colonies of over 200 birds. This fellow was a loner and not a common species for our area. Like me. I reflected on all that we had in common.

That duck lived on the lake for almost a year, completely content with me pulling up my boat every Sunday to peer into his nest and take his picture. He became my inspiration and guide to the acceptance of being alone.

After many months of despair, one of my granddaughters called, inviting me to join her and her husband on a cruise to Europe. The trip was timely, and I dared to believe this might bring me back to some joy and laughter, the two emotions that were so reminiscent of life with Tino.

Before I left Lake Ilopango, I checked in with Tino again through another session with Deborah and told him about the upcoming journey. He replied, "Well, even though I've already been to Italy several times with you, I guess I will go again with you guys. But don't think that just because I am dead I'm going to museums!" (Something he deplored.) He also bragged about not having to pack a suitcase or go through a pat-down by the TSA now that he was traveling "light."

During this session he reminded Deborah and me many times that he was now intact. He pointed to his feet and insisted that she tell me that they were no longer cut off and that he did not need a wheelchair to move around. He was impressed at how he could just think of a place and project himself there with no travel required.

It was the same when he wanted to be with me. He would think of me and instantly be next to me. This new-found skill allowed him to be on vacation with me, but also to be back at the house to check on things. He took great delight in being in two places at the same time.

During the session Tino showed up again in his fifties. He appeared very well dressed and jokingly reminded

Deborah that he never showed up for our sessions in the same outfit twice. This was a jab at me for my insistence on the impeccability of his wardrobe. Deborah laughed when on one occasion Tino showed up young, vibrant, in his late twenties, and when she described him to me, I had no idea whom she was talking about. We finally figured out it was Tino in an attempt at showing off.

CHAPTER TEN

I ARRIVED IN ROME WHERE I would spend a few days before joining Tiffany on the cruise. I hired an amazing guide to show me around, and she managed to get me an opportunity to visit the Sistine Chapel alone. I stood in awe of being in this much-visited place in quiet solitude, especially since fifteen minutes later I knew that roughly 20,000 people would be showing up.

I lay down on the floor, which none of the guards seemed to care about, and looked up at the middle of the ceiling, seeing God there with his white beard, reaching out to Adam to impart the spark of life to him in the fresco "Creation of Adam." I was intrigued by the fact that God was depicted inside a brain-like sphere. This was a backdrop for my sense that the mind is from the source of God and a common vibration that permeates through us. Our mind and soul combined form our channel to God.

Tino was right, we never die.

Next, I spotted the Libyan Sibyl, a woman prophet who could see into the future and predicted the coming of Jesus

Christ. What a surprise to see a psychic represented on the ceiling of the Sistine Chapel!

I glanced at a fig tree in the Garden of Eden and saw Satan depicted as a snake, and was sorely disappointed that its head was depicted as female.

Finally, I turned to see the front fresco, with its vivid colors portraying the Last Judgment and the resurrection of the dead. On the left side of this fresco, I looked into heaven and saw angels playing their trumpets trying to pull people up into the clouds. On the right, more angels, apparently male, were beating up spirits and trying to keep them all in hell. In the center of it all was Christ in all of his judging and glory. I tried to process the scene, as it had taken on a new meaning for me now that Tino had transitioned. Lastly, I saw a figure of a man with donkey ears and a snake wrapped around his body. In the snake's mouth was his penis. At that point, I'd had enough of the Christian version of heaven and hell and left the chapel.

These images were a major contrast to my experience of Tino going to the other side and wanting to have a casual chat about his to-do list. Although the images and paintings were breathtaking in their visual impact, there was so much fear in the eyes of the bodies portrayed there. The scene of hell was chaotic, painting death as a gruesome and violent event. It validated even more my unwillingness to believe that the energy of Christ could be attached to that thinking.

My next stop in Rome was the Borghese Gallery. After I passed through several rooms of art, I reached the far corner of the building where Bernini's statue of Apollo and Daphne stands. Apollo is struck by Cupid's arrow and is moving forward, trying to capture Daphne, who is turning into a tree. It was like having what you want in your hands and watching it slip away. Turning one form into another, flesh going back to earth.

I had so many metaphors to take with me. Would I now see everything in my world through the lens of losing someone?

A couple of days later I met Tiffany and her husband, Nick, and we arrived at the cruise ship. I wanted so much to share with her the remarkable experiences with her grandfather since his death and the conversations Tino and I had been having through Deborah. Sharing that, however, was a real challenge, as I had no idea whether she would be open to these possibilities.

We decided to go for a cup of coffee and Tiff ordered a frozen coffee drink. I carefully broke the news of the relationship I was having with her grandfather on the other side. At first she was skeptical, but at the same time hopeful that what I was saying was true. It wasn't easy sharing the unknown and unseen with others, and although it went rather well, I returned to my cabin unsure of the impact it had made. I powered up my phone and there was a message from Deborah.

"Tino stopped by my office a bit ago. Maybe you can explain to me why I have the taste of frozen coffee in my mouth."

I stared at the text in disbelief. Could it be possible to validate what was happening in a text from Deborah with a message from the other side?

A few days into the cruise, we were off to a port in Greece. The previous evening there had been some confusion about Tiff and Nick and I eating in the same dining room, since they had an inside room and I was in a balcony suite. We were frustrated with the process and complained, but got no satisfactory response from management.

While on a shore excursion another text message came in from Deborah saying, "Tino wants his grandkids to travel in style and he is working on it." The kids read the message with quizzical looks, but we all knew that if Tino was in charge, anything was possible.

We arrived back at the ship, and fifteen minutes later I had a call from the concierge urging me to go to the front desk. The manager wanted to talk to me. I listened as he apologized for the mix up at the dining room and handed me a key to a balcony suite for Tiff and Nick—at no additional charge.

In five minutes their bags were packed and unpacked and they were sitting on their new private deck looking out over the Mediterranean Sea! I sat with them on their balcony celebrating their upgrade with a glass of wine and wondering how Tino had pulled it off.

The following evening Tiff wanted to go to the karaoke competition, so we headed out. There were quite a few singers with song choices mostly from the pop charts. The last singer to perform was a man from Mexico who would be performing in Spanish. The music began and the screen started displaying the lyrics as he belted out the first few words. Suddenly, looking completely confused, he asked that the song be stopped. However, it continued to play, even while his microphone dangled in his hand. The song was "El Rey," the same song we played when we spread Tino's ashes on the rocks at the lake.

This was obviously not what the man had planned to sing. He looked at the DJ with frustration as he frantically pushed buttons to reprogram his choice. The master of ceremonies took the microphone, apologizing for some "technical difficulties." My granddaughter and I were laughing hysterically on the couch, without saying anything to each other. We knew it was Tino having a great time behind the scenes! I lay in bed that night and marveled at everything Tino was capable of, even though in my stubbornness I still wanted to put it in the "coincidence file."

With the Italy adventure behind me, I decided to plan another trip, this time to Miami. I stated my purpose clearly to Tino, challenging him to speak to me directly. I had read that butterflies were the most often-mentioned sign from those on the other side, so I figured I would start trying to make the connection through a physical form. Surely Tino could make a butterfly appear because he had done so well with that big duck. Since Tino never did anything in a small way, I knew he would make a clear statement and not disappoint.

While on the plane to Miami, it occurred to me that 30,000-feet high might be the perfect place to attempt a conversation with him, assuming he was "up" in heaven. I was learning that with telepathy I could send my thoughts out into the energy field of the universe where Tino would pick up on them and appear.

I sent out on the spiritual airways to Tino that we needed to chat. Much to my surprise, I very quickly felt his swooping in again and the quiet conversation in my mind began. "Tino, here is the deal. I want to see butterflies. The more the merrier."

I kept asking Tino for more proof that we were speaking, each instance further breaking down the barriers of my belief that I could interact with someone on the other side.

I got to my rental car in Miami, and while I was waiting to exit the parking lot a song called "Mariposa" came on the radio. *Mariposa* is the Spanish word for a butterfly.

I almost missed the relevance, but when an impression from Tino would come to me it heightened my senses so I could hear the words to the song louder and clearer. As I listened to it, I couldn't help smiling. Things were going well, and he was certainly engaged with my request.

When I arrived at my hotel and called my friend Karla to confirm where we would meet for lunch the next day, she, of course, suggested a restaurant called Mariposa. I barely stumbled through the rest of the conversation, elated by the validating message.

The next day, eager to get to Mariposa, I arrived early. The restaurant was on the second floor of Neiman Marcus in Coral Gables. I made my way through the counters of purses and perfumes towards the escalator. I stopped in my tracks, however, when I looked up and saw a cascade of at least a thousand white butterflies attached to strings with little mirrors hanging down from the ceiling! It was an enchanting sight with all the lights glittering off of the mirrors, and I was truly struck by the wonder of it all. It was the most amazing gift I ever received from Tino. No possession on Earth could have been as captivating as that moment!

I stepped on the escalator as if I was ascending into a galactic realm, which was a far cry from the front altar of the Sistine Chapel. All that was missing was Led Zeppelin's "Stairway to Heaven"!

At the top of the escalator I could no longer hold back the outpouring of emotions I was feeling. I settled on a nearby bench and the tears flowed. A concerned salesperson asked if I was all right, and since there were no words for what had just happened, I simply shook my head yes, while at the same time hearing a distant voice saying, "Lori, be careful what you ask for." In a kind gesture, the woman handed me **a small carton of water with butterflies on it.**

After lunch I was alone looking for some cosmetics, moving from counter to counter perusing foundations, lipsticks, and face treatments. I gathered my few purchases, paid, and started digging for the keys to the rental car.

First round, nothing appeared, so it was time to do the full evacuation of all items. I spread my belongings on the glass case in front of me and still came up with no keys. Turning the purse upside down and shaking every last bit of debris on the marble floors resulted again in—nothing. Panic started to invade my perfect "mariposa" moment. Great! I had locked my cell phone in the car and now the keys were nowhere to be found. I went counter by counter, searching for them, and then engaged all the salespeople to join in. High and low we looked until one of the young women finally held up the keys and triumphantly said, "Got 'em!"

By this time the impact of the butterflies had faded as I was back in surviving-widow mode. I went to the car, happy to see my phone there, and took a quick peek at my messages. An urgent message from Deborah read, "Lori, Tino says do not lose the key to the rental car. It will be a pain in the ass to get another one."

With my cell phone in my hand, I leaned against the headrest and another torrent of tears came tumbling down my face. These tears broke through all the barriers of protection I had built around me, thinking that those who left were never to be seen or heard from again. It also turned out to be a release and actualization of a gift I had brought into the world as a child so many years before. I knew deep inside that all of this was possible and that it was a natural state for me to communicate with the other side.

The folder I had filed so many "coincidental" events in was now marked "empty."

Today, I look back on the escalator ride and realize that it was a metaphor for the steps I have taken in awakening into the knowledge that spirits are very much alive and well and living on the other side!

CHAPTER ELEVEN

I WAS BACK IN EL Salvador again, continuing with my personal damage assessments. My separation from Tino made
me realize that most of the world familiar to me when Tino
was alive, no longer existed. Shallow family relationships
and friendships crumble when you are no longer married,
and business associations diminish when the power of the
couple is gone. With the stopping of one man's breath, my
world, as I had known it, was gone.

The beautiful home that we meticulously built seven
years earlier to house our dreams had now become an empty
box. As I packed Tino's clothing and some other personal
items to donate to charities, I realized possessions have no
energy other than what we give them. Who really cared
what label was on the back of Tino's silk ties now? The
stylish, perfectly laundered dress shirts hung in the closet in
strikingly helpless poses. All the specially designed orthope-
dic shoes no longer needed to wait for their next steps, because now none would come. Truly my accumulation mode
had come to a skidded halt.

I revisited a stack of sympathy cards from members of El Salvador's high society and realized that their empathy for my loss was really a *bon voyage*. Each card almost shouted a farewell to my past, announcing that my time in society had expired.

Waiting to fill that emptiness, I was lost and alone with myself, yet it was not a tragic loss. This would be my point of departure into the world of the unseen and a captivating adventure.

Saying I was beginning to go through a spiritual awakening doesn't quite define what was happening to me, since in fact, there are as many definitions of awakening as there are actual awakenings. This phenomenon is not to be confused with a conversion, such as when a person converts to a new religion or is "born again." Religious conversion is the acceptance of a new set of beliefs and dogma. I was not converting to a new belief system. I was destroying the old beliefs that had become obstacles to my growth.

My ego had begun to dissolve. This did not mean I felt I was right and that everyone else was wrong. I simply no longer found value in entertaining a lack of truth and impeccability.

I was still broken, empty, and devastated at times because of the loss of what I once thought was relevant, but my need for belonging to anything was shifting. Although I was losing my societal connections, my existence was strangely that of being a part of everything and everyone around me. Who would have thought that I, the left-brained, practical entrepreneur, would ever utter the words *I was becoming one with the universe,* but that actually describes what happened. With this shift and the battle through all the trauma and turmoil, I was now in a state of burgeoning enlightenment.

It was almost a year since Tino died. I went to my office after my now mandatory morning meditation that had been suggested by Deborah. There was, on my desk, an old book my mother had given to me when I was a child. Oddly, here it was laying front and center on my desk, Alice's Adventures in Wonderland, published in 1946, well before I was born. On the cover was a very wet Alice swimming in a lake with a rat. I began reading it and found it easy to relate to Alice's struggles to adapt to odd new rules and the strange behaviors of adults. What I didn't realize at the time was that Alice's story was a metaphor for how shamans go "down the rabbit hole" into the spiritual realm known as the lower world of existence.

The lower world is the realm of our ancestors and spirits. This is the dimension where the power of the Earth and its elements reside together with the deepest aspect of the soul, our thoughts, and our emotions. Traveling into the lower world is a sacred journey for shamans as it is here that they retrieve their power through altered states of consciousness and merge with the animal spirits that have become their guides.

I had no awareness that I had arrived at this door and was peeking through the keyhole at these things.

My office overlooked a garden full of flowers and, on this particular morning, still wondering how the book landed on my desk, I ventured outside and held a bright red hibiscus flower larger than my hand. Suddenly the flower dissolved before my eyes. Then my hand dissolved—and I felt the same sensation as I had once years earlier while standing on the peninsula overlooking Lake Ilopango of my cells melding into my environment. I looked around, wondering what had caused me to shift, and I was alone. My mind kept struggling to make sense of it. I was becoming very much like Alice, shrinking into the wholeness of all that was around me.

Moments later I brushed off the incident and grabbed a cup of coffee. Slowly, life was becoming a wonderland of experiences that my soul knew existed and my mind had so long denied.

I reflected on the year that had passed. I was still feeling shortchanged since after talking with Tino it seemed he had avoided grief and pain and been set free in some way. I felt left behind. He was on his way to higher levels of consciousness while I was stuck in the gravity of my body with my painful thoughts. I also felt disabled, as if Tino had taken a piece of my soul with him. It wasn't fair that I had given him his last breath on earth, yet now he seemed so much more alive than me as I was always just trying to keep my head above water in an ocean of grief.

There were some moments when the clouds of despair would evaporate and I would be happy for Tino, telling myself that it was his time to leave his decaying limbs and dance in all the enlightenment and discovery he was experiencing. I tried to be unselfish and celebrate his newfound wholeness, but the clouds would return and all I could think about was that he was not dancing with me.

I wanted to know his perspective, as I knew it would enrich mine. I felt that only then could we both enjoy that great and wonderful ride into our new selves. It was time to talk to Tino again and I spent a lot of time before the session considering the questions I would ask.

We had often talked about the spiritual side of things when he was here on Earth. During our marriage I had been a spiritual curiosity seeker wanting to know more about our existence on some level after we transitioned. Tino, however, had been very skeptical of my ventures into the mystical world. He would tease me when I had a tarot card reading done and for thinking that psychics might be authentic.

Now it was time for the million-dollar "I told you so." Okay, I admit, there was a selfish streak to my inquiry, but it was begging to be asked. "So, Tino," I started, "you were quite the skeptic about psychics and all the other spiritual woo-woo I would share with you. What do you think now about the fact that we are having a chat?" I truly wore the grin of the Cheshire cat on my face.

There was a long pause, and then he sucked it up and responded. "Okay, I cannot believe this is happening. On Earth, I never thought it was possible. I thought all of this was nonsense. "

Deborah then described Tino rolling a piece of paper into a ball and throwing it into the garbage. She said, "This means he thought it was a bunch of garbage."

Tino continued, "Yes, Lori, I was a skeptic then, but I'll be damned, it is real. Lori, you should see all the spirits here. They are everywhere! You are going to really like it here. You've got to see this place and imagine how much fun we will have. The possibilities are endless. Okay, okay, I admit it. I honestly had never thought this was possible. Damn if you did not prove me wrong!"

Tino went on, "I know that when Lori gets off the phone she is going to be laughing her head off. She will probably want to throw a party to celebrate that she was right. I feel kind of silly now not to have believed this was possible, but it is. I'm finding that much on the spiritual side is very surprising.

CHAPTER TWELVE

IN LATIN AMERICA, AN emphasis is placed on commemorating the first anniversary of someone's passing. With Tino's daughter Carolina and her family visiting me from the States, I decided to host a small celebration.

I scheduled a session with Deborah and Tino for the morning of the party.

When I asked for his input about the party, the first thing out of Tino's mouth was "fireworks," but then he realized my heart was nowhere near a fireworks show. "I know there will be moments that will be harder than others, and quite honestly, I do not want to go there. I am also going through a grieving process although it's very different from yours. I go to the rocks in the lake and stand there, feeling like I am in the center of life. I can see all around and have the experience of a physical being. There is nostalgia for the land, the lake, and the people I loved. Although I have a memory of us living at the lake together, I look now upon it with different eyes. I do not feel the pain of losing you, as you are never lost to me."

The session ended, the guests arrived, and I headed down the stairs to the dock with the same box that had held Tino's ashes a year ago. This time the box was full of sleeping butterflies that were to be awakened and set free in his honor. Tino's brother and his wife and some nieces and nephews joined me and we all went out in the boat to the rocks as I had done so many times that year. A silly thought came through about how my husband was now residing out there with the duck. It was a somber time as the butterflies were released, and we all remembered Tino. In keeping with tradition we ended up back in the pool. Later that afternoon Tino's daughter came running to me in the house and said, "Hurry, you will not believe it!"

I ran to the front lawn and looked out over the lake towards the rocks, and there it was again! I stood in awe at the sight of a huge rainbow, even bigger than the one before. I asked myself, *Lori, just how many signs do you need?*

Carolina and her family went back to Arizona and one of my granddaughters who would be starting college later stayed behind. By this time, I accepted that I was actually able to hear and communicate with spirits. I did not, however, fully trust what I was hearing. There was often a constant ringing in my ears, like a radio inside my head was being tuned to a remote station.

I was enjoying the last days with my granddaughter sitting on the patio and welcoming the breeze coming over the lake. Strangely, with the wind also came a steady drumming beat. I listened as the drumming continued. Since my ears were becoming so sensitive to sounds, I asked my granddaughter to come outside to listen. She heard it too.

I thought it was strange after fifteen years of living at the lake that I had never heard this drumming before. Could we both be hearing things? I grabbed my granddaughter and got in the boat to visit some of the small communities around the lake, to see if they were the source of the drumming. Everywhere we went, the answer was no, and it was accompanied by puzzled looks that suggested we might be a little crazy for asking.

A few days later, my granddaughter went home to the United States. I was alone again.

I knew I was going through some kind of metamorphosis. I was seeing spirits now regularly. I was feeling and hearing them. I also continued to hear the drumming. It became a kind of joke with me. Walking out of the house, the drums would start. Going inside, the drums would stop. Start, stop, start, stop! It continued on. The sound had an ancient, indigenous feeling to it.

A couple weeks later I was startled in the middle of the night by a cyclone of energy encircling my body. It had actually lifted me off the bed! My entire body was floating! The event was unnerving, yet amazing. The following night, I came to an awareness that I was flying into my bedroom as if I had been traveling. Then, I would wake up with memories of being deep in the inner world below the lake with a large civilization of ancient Mayans. There was just too much happening that couldn't be explained for me to ignore it, but I knew that if I shared these experiences others might say I was "out of my mind" with grief.

I tried to do normal, work-related things, but extraordinary things continued to happen. A large boa constrictor showed up on the patio and had to be removed. Another very venomous snake was slithering around the front door of the house. Day after day we were removing snakes. The last straw was when I was sitting in my office and another boa constrictor dropped down in front of the glass doors with a dove in its mouth!

I knew it was not a normal occurrence to have that many snakes around, so I called Deborah to discuss what this meant. She was impressed with my story since snakes are powerful signs from the spirit world. Because they cast off their old skin periodically, they represent rebirth or renewal, serving as a metaphor for releasing old ways of being.

I also learned from Deborah's spirit guides that the power of the snake represents vital energy that waits coiled in our spine in the sacrum, a triangular bone at the base of the torso, above the tailbone. The energy, which many people know as *kundalini,* stays there until it is ready to move. For the Mayans and many other ancient cultures, the movement of this energy from the sacrum into the heart is a recognized symptom of awakening, as it fuses the masculine and feminine energy inside us, and leads to full enlightenment. For the Mayans this concept is embodied in the symbol of a snake and described as koyopa ("lightning") in the blood and its movement is called *the path of the feathered serpent.*

I then began to hear messages from what seemed to be ancient Mayan spirits. They told me I had come to Central America because of some kind of karmic destiny and made reference to a deep connection my soul had with them during a past life. Day by day I received a download of information that I wasn't sure about since the information I got came to me in pieces. All I knew was that I was feeling tremendous empathy for the indigenous people in El Salvador regarding the inequities and persecution that they had endured.

On a particular day, the skies were clear and the spirits instructed me to stand on the lawn in front of the house, which I did. Maria and Carmen were watching me from the kitchen window, since they shared a growing concern at seeing me walk around the house talking to myself (as they saw it). "Wait here," the voices said, and I did. While I waited, the drumming was persistent and more forceful than usual. Suddenly, a little cloud appeared over me and dumped a torrential amount of rain. I could feel the drops around me, but not on me. Stunned, I returned to the house and stood in the living room.

Maria came into the room and said, "Senora, we saw you under the rain cloud!" Then noticing my dry clothes, she exclaimed, "Oh, my god! Why aren't you wet?"

Speechless, I simply turned and walked away. I had no words to describe what had just happened.

The next day, which was the day before my fifty-second birthday, the spirit voices wanted me to go to the point at the end of the peninsula that night. They would be sending me more information and a very special gift from the spirit world. Oddly, I was not afraid. My earth mind was less dominant as I was starting to realize that I could shift my awareness of other dimensions and hear spirit voices very clearly now.

What I did not know was the significance of the fifty-second birthday. For the Mayans, the date was viewed as a milestone in a person's life because two Mayan calendars synchronize on this date. What this means is that you have finished your first life cycle and it is time for a rebirth. The Mayans saw this as the beginning of a transformational period during which you would become a tribal elder and accept the role of mentoring others. People who survive to this age were considered to hold great wisdom. The process of transitioning into this role in their culture lasted for roughly two years. Some Mayans would sacrifice their lives to the gods when they reached fifty-two, hoping the gods would smile upon their descendants. This was considered an honorable suicide.

Before it was dark, the spirit voices told me to step outside and I gazed across the lake where I saw clouds of smoke rising out of the jungle around the lake—as if some kind of a ceremony was being prepared.

After guiding me to my closet, the spirits showed me exactly what to wear. The end of the peninsula was a good distance from the house, so Edgardo helped me take a chair, a pitcher of water, a glass, and my cell phone with me as we headed down.

I told the staff not to come to me unless I called them, and then I sat in the darkness under the near-full moon, listening to soft voices speaking in an unfamiliar language. I heard footsteps—but saw no one. I felt certain though, that spirits were gathering around me.

I was urged to stand with my arms outstretched, as a huge surge of wind came up from the south and moved through me! My silk blouse fluttered like the wings of a butterfly. Any fear of what might happen had been reduced to almost nothing and I felt a remarkable sense that I was in the perfect place and time. There was a sense of destiny.

Then, as instructed, I lay down on the grass. At that moment, I knew something very sacred and life changing was about to happen. I was not wrong.

Shamans are connected to elements of their landscape, especially mountains and bodies of water. I could sense the center of the volcano, as if the power of lava below the lake was growing and bubbling underneath me. My own energy continued to be carried on a crescendo of the breeze that was flowing as I realized in that moment that I was not of this world. My soul was being infused into the rocks that were submerged beneath the lake. My mind had long since "disappeared" and was no longer available as I gazed up and saw colorful lights passing above me.

I lifted my arm, pointing my finger into the sky toward the moon, so I could touch it. I poked its surface and it moved. Each time I touched the moon, my hands would emit a glow. And again—a glow! And again—a glow!

The stars were pulsing in a magical rhythm, and the moon was elegant in her swirling silky pattern. The moment was mesmerizing, with the drum beat of the universe and the melting lava. Gently, I lowered my arm back to the soft grass and my body began to melt into the soil. Blades of grass started rising around me as I sank into the earth—the rest of me crumbling into pieces of total bliss. The only sensory piece left was my eyes. The moon shifted and energy seemed to spill out of it, forming a funnel of light which came directly at me with blinding speed, spearing its way into my body.

I do not recall what happened after the beam of light entered my body.

★ ★ ★

Over twenty years before I found myself lying at the end of that peninsula, I had visited a shaman in the Arizona desert with my good friend Barbara. She had always enjoyed discovering the mystical in the world, and since I was open to those possibilities I was a perfect friend to have tag along.

We arrived at a sparsely populated area with a few doublewide trailers parked on it. Soon we were inside one of these and sitting in the shaman's living room, listening as he spoke of his gifts. His cat approached me and was on my lap in seconds, apparently eager to bask in the energy I was exuding. The shaman's eyes opened wide and he tipped his head in curiosity, watching the interaction between his cat and me. He stood up, pointed to another room, and asked me to follow him.

I stood in front of him and he asked me to place my palms face up. Then he placed his over mine. As if energy was jolting out of me, he lifted his hands abruptly and said in a startled voice, "You are a healer. You have the gift. And what are you doing here in Arizona? Why are you living here? You are not in the right place. You are Mayan. You are a shaman and need to be with your people. You must go back to Central America where you belong!"

The shaman then gifted me a bowl of rocks, saying they were magical, powerful, and held the creative power of the universe. He emphasized his confidence that I could heal people, and encouraged me to start using my hands for healing. As he accompanied us to the door, he placed his hands on my shoulder and said, "Someday you will discover who you really are. Trust me." I left his home with more questions than I had arrived with.

In the car on the way back, Barbara and I were rather baffled by the whole experience. Although we wanted to believe him in some way, the idea of me being a healer seemed pretty far out. First of all, I had made no mention of any connection to Central America, which at that point was simply my Salvadoran boyfriend. Second, I was not at all knowledgeable or immersed in indigenous cultures or new age thinking.

Could this have been the precursor of what had just happened to me at the lake?

★ ★ ★

My cell phone beeped, which coaxed me back to where my body was lying on the grass at the lake. I wiggled my fingers and toes, then turned my head enough to glance at my phone and was surprised to find that I had been laying there for three hours. Where in the hell had I been during that time? I had no idea. I tried to get up, but felt paralyzed. I later learned that I had symptoms of astral catalepsy, which is the body's response to extreme emotional shock due to an out-of-body experience.

I finally garnered enough strength to move my legs and stood up. I looked out over the lake, hoping to catch a glimpse of something that would explain what had just happened. As I gazed around, I realized that when I looked at lights, I saw triangles everywhere. It was as if a magical pair of glasses had been placed over my eyes so I could navigate a behind-scenes view of what was going on among the forces of energy in everything. Then, triangles began to connect to one another and in the process all things became connected—like a spider web was forming around me—with threads reaching out to other geometric figures that formed an even larger grid.

This experience finally destroyed the reality I knew and trusted. There were no words; I could not speak. I went back to the house and to my bedroom where all of the cats were sleeping, waiting for me on the bed. I was wondering if I was really even on Earth, as I felt as if I was floating. I petted the cats, hoping they were even really there, and was relieved that I could feel their fur.

The next morning, I needed to process what had happened to me, but I had no idea where to start. There was not a hotline in the world that would understand my call. Dazed, I walked to my office to see if "normal" existed anywhere and I realized that I had a meeting scheduled that day in the city. I was on the board of directors of a foundation that Tino and I had started to support environmental and social causes at the lake, so I drove forty-five minutes into the city to attend the board meeting.

From fear of what might come out of my mouth, I remained quiet and listened while others spoke of concerns about dwindling donations. I finally told the board members they should stop worrying about raising money since I could now see into the future and knew that everything would be okay. There were several raised eyebrows and strange grins, and I went quiet again. Feeling like I could not tell the difference between present, past, and future, and hearing spirits chime in with their commentary on everything, I realized it was extremely complicated to be in a normal environment that required a logical mind.

On the way home I passed the same makeshift houses I had seen hundreds of times. This time, however, the depth of my compassion for other beings was greater than anything I had felt before. I could sense the misery of others. I could feel the depth of pain from the Earth for the degradation it had endured. The sight of garbage was like a knife piercing my heart. The pain and suffering of all those around me rose like a smoky fire within my body. Sadness and frustration seeped into my soul, and I thought I might be erupting from the feeling of needing, personally, to purge all that was wrong in the world.

I was exhausted. What would happen now that I go back to the scene of this exceptional event? I guessed that I would need to try to embrace what had happened and somehow make sense of what it would now bring.

Everything I perceived had many more dimensions than I could have imagined. The depth and intensity of every object was a treacherous journey, as my mind climbed over shapes and sizes I had never seen before. I later realized I was seeing things in the realm of sacred geometry.

I would move further and further away from the earth dimension as my soul dove deeper into the depths of discovery to what was behind the veil of our existence. I could see the past as vividly as the future, and being present meant simply floating in the wonder of it all.

This new existence kept me in a trance-like state. I sensed my isolation as I moved through a world no one else could see. I felt so detached that I would walk into the kitchen and stand in front of Maria and Carmen determined to find out if they could even see me. Only after they acknowledged me would I turn and walk away, with a feeling of relief that I was still there.

When I finally slept, it was intensely deep, and I was still traveling outside of my body because I would wake to find myself coming through my bedroom window to merge with it again. By now I was regularly visiting the Mayans under the lake.

Spirits would awaken me at 4:00 a.m., a time that seemed to be when the transmission of their messages was the easiest. They were teaching me the healing and divination practices that are the basics of shamanism. I would get out of bed, feeling there was a spirit inside of me. If I let myself just be, the being inside would move my legs and arms and slowly walk within me. If I moved too fast I would leave it behind, so my movements became very deliberate. I had to find a way for my mind to step aside and let the spirit move me. I was guided to certain objects—the spirit providing greater focus on them through my eyes—and I could see the energy associated with each particular item. The spirit would lift my hands and grab the object for me. This walk through the house would have looked to an observer like I was doing tai chi, as my movements became in sync with the entity inside of me.

Each object chosen was placed on the coffee table. A flower, a picture, words cut from magazines, pieces of jewelry, photos—all were placed in some kind of planned grid that became my altar. Each object held a particular energy, and when they were all placed together, I had created a powerful energy grid for my protection.

The spirit voices continued to share ancient wisdom and knowledge of sacred ways. This initiation continued day after day. I never really questioned the why in all of it, as my rational, linear mind was no longer the authoritative voice in the process.

One of the most difficult lessons was when the spirits asked me to go outside to the large cage I had built to house my African love birds. They told me to go inside the cage and sit there. While in the cage I could see the little houses I had put in for each of the pairs, as well as the small bowls of fruit and vegetables. The spirits said sternly, "Experience the world from this place, caged and confined. They have no freedom. You have taken away their ability to survive." I was swamped in such sorrow for what I had done that, placing my head in my hands, I wept for almost an hour huddled in the corner of the cage.

I was starting to see visions, as if the spirits were sending them to me. While sitting in the cage they showed me visions of blue macaws in cages, and soon I was opening the doors to set them free—until at last I saw a multitude of them, delightfully and freely swarming around me like they had on the day I married Tino.

It seemed a perfect storm had brought me to this place. The most commonly occurring image in my visions was of a mysterious and charismatic male figure wearing an ornate headdress of blue and yellow macaw feathers. Whenever I would see this man I would get a very peculiar feeling about his essence. Just when I thought he would reveal his face, however, he always turned in a way that it could not be seen.

When the man walked among thousands of Mayans, he stood taller than most, which made me suspect he represented Tino in some way. Parts of this man's headdress were decorated with gemstones, pearls and a fuchsia-colored stone I would later learn was pink tourmaline. This particular stone carried a mesmerizing energy whenever I would stare into it.

I could also see and feel the presence of four jaguar spirits around this man, as they took up positions in the four directions. They resembled leopards. Their coats were tan and dotted with black rosettes. I sensed the man had a connection to the lake. Often I asked the spirits about this man's identity, but my question was never answered.

The jaguars around the spirit of the man would communicate with me at times, and when I asked them about the source of information being downloaded to me, they told me it came from a place in the Milky Way that should be familiar to me.

There was an odd feeling that I had a relationship with these creatures, so in some way it felt comforting to hear them and receive their thoughts in my mind. They gave me the impression that since I had been blasted open, I was vulnerable and required "spiritual body guards" to walk safely in the world. Since I felt like a walking light bulb, the presence of the jaguars was welcome.

I was feeling the potential of attracting a multitude of energies—both good and not so good—as the voices I heard varied and I had no idea of the source of the information I was hearing.

I was also obsessed with being barefoot. I guess I needed grounding. Putting on shoes seemed very strange to me even as I stared at the fifty pairs of shoes in my closet. I walked barefoot in the garden, which was—because of my new, heightened perception—beyond enchanting. Stepping into the dark, rich volcanic soil around my house, I would begin digging with my toes until my feet were submerged up to my ankles. The feeling of the dirt was ecstasy, as its nutrients seemed to calm the firecracker-like sensation shooting off at the edges of my nervous system.

I also sensed that I was morphing. Every morning I gazed in the mirror with curiosity, trying to see beyond my skin and into my eyes—in search of who I really was inside. Everything I had thought I was, I was becoming less of.

In this state I felt an abundance of love that I had not felt since Tino died. There was surprise in everything I saw as I walked through my property, swept up by the beauty: Busy insects became moving highways as they formed part of the larger scene of everything making their contribution to the whole; trees started to echo stories with words that found true synchronicity and resonance in my being. At times I would become so lost in the experience of nature that my mind would interrupt me to question if it was real. After being transported to a world others could not perceive, I would head back to the kitchen for another reality check with Maria and Carmen.

Since the phenomena I was experiencing were so difficult for the rational mind to grasp, I would reach points of total disbelief and ask my newfound spirit guides to prove things in more concrete terms through cause and effect. Obliging me, on one occasion they took me out to a spot on the edge of the property overlooking the lake and spoke to me of a beautiful white bird quite a distance away. They said to think of it, and it would come to me. I concentrated on the bird until it appeared in my mind. It looked like a large crane. Then I opened my eyes and searched the distant shore to see if the bird would actually appear. Suddenly the wind picked up forcefully like an approaching storm. The trees blew violently and debris swirled around me, but I kept my gaze fixed on the other side of the lake until, amazed, I saw the white bird flapping its wings and flying toward me.

The bird landed on the grass near my feet. I stood in awe and realized that an alchemical storm had rewired me and shifted me into a higher vibration, dramatically affecting what I could manifest.

Another unforgettable experience occurred when I was sitting on the patio having breakfast and watching a few butterflies flittering around the flowers. Within a few moments there were hundreds of butterflies swarming around me—so many that I could hardly see the plate that held my breakfast. The next day a similar thing occurred. When I focused on some dragonflies, their numbers dramatically multiplied too. Maria and Carmen were stunned at what they too were witnessing around me. We all were amazed by how any living creatures I would focus on would increase in number and appear in exaggerated ways.

After a week of living like this, I finally questioned the meaning of it all. Why? I started to ask the voices, and explanations began to come in images as clear as a high definition movie, yet always as misunderstood as starting to watch a movie in the middle of its plot.

The Mayan leader with the blue-feathered headdress also continued to be part of a recurring scene I kept seeing. He was directing the movements of a rather panic-stricken group of Mayans during the time when the Spanish had come to Central America. There were Mayans running all around him trying to hide treasures and valuables by throwing them into shallow bodies of water. This scene explains why one night, in a trance, I gathered up all my jewelry and started walking toward the lake to "hide" my treasures in its watery depths.

Thank God, Maria intercepted me. After a bout of convincing me that my jewelry was in safekeeping in case the Spanish came, I finally returned to bed.

It was now almost two weeks since the incident on the point when I was catapulted out of my body and I was completely immersed in a world no one else could see or hear. At night I continued to hear the drums and smell fires that were not present in ordinary reality, but which were very real in the nonordinary reality I was experiencing. I would catch the essence of copal, a tree resin the Mayans used as incense, lingering in the breezes. This stirred a remembering in me that felt very welcome.

I closed my eyes in hope of more images of understanding and there he was again—the Mayan leader—sitting in front of a large fire with others huddled around him. As usual, all I could see were the yellow and hyacinth macaw feathers of his headdress. But this time there were the faces of others, painted with brilliant yellows, greens, and fuchsias. The textiles the Mayans wore were magnificent, and I could sense the intensity of the dyes that had brought those colors to such a brilliant state.

As the energy of the lake serenaded me, I stared into the fire in a deep feeling of community with the spirits who were present, almost wanting to jump into that vision and claim my own seat by that fire. My eyes remained closed and I watched, as the scene grew more intense due to the incessant beat of the drums and the fire's growing heat.

The earthly heartbeat started again and echoed across the lake, into my ears, as it had done when I was on the point. Soon I was behind my eyelids, watching as the leader stretched out his arms and lifted them into the sky as he started to cry out in a tone which seemed so familiar to me, in words I completely understood.

I continued to watch with great anticipation as he slowly turned his head in my direction and the feathers fell back on his shoulder—finally allowing me to see his face with the fire reflecting on it.

And there, looking straight into the face of this ancient Mayan leader, the face I saw staring back at me was my own.

CHAPTER THIRTEEN

I WOKE UP THE NEXT day with more questions than answers.
Who was I? Really? What was this Mayan leader doing
with my face? What did I have to do with all of this, anyway?

A few times I started thinking about the significance
of my role in that early lifetime, and in an odd way found I
was actually comfortable with those thoughts until my ego
took over. Any marveling at the potential of who I was or
basking in the grandiosity of my previous importance would
quickly result in hearing the footsteps of one of my cats
heading for the litter box. Soon I would hear the scratching
and moving of sand to cover fresh poop.

This was a clear message I was receiving from spirit
urging me to stay out the ego—and clean out the cat box!
I will admit this happened more than once, to the point
where I wondered if my cats had some kind of transistor in
them that sounded a silent alarm any time my ego was out
of whack.

After realizing that this powerful Mayan must have
been me in a previous lifetime, I knew that not accepting this

knowledge in less than a humble way would not serve me in what was obviously becoming some sort of initiation process.

I had honestly never been curious about Mayan prophecies. Now I was coming to the realization that I was somehow involved in something far beyond what any part of me in this lifetime could understand. It was a far greater story than my own.

I was still on a merry-go-round of heightened energy, which grew harder to get off every day. There were times I would actually collapse from lack of sleep or just from mere exhaustion, and perhaps needless to say, I was taking a very hard look at my sanity. The beam of light that had struck my body had blasted me wide open, making me oversensitive to sounds, smells, touch, taste, and sight. This condition was becoming overwhelming to manage.

One day, all the electronics in the house started beaming signals into my psyche and the screeching sound I heard was unbearable. My computer vibrated with so much energy I could no longer navigate to or from the websites I sought. Certain buttons appeared to be pulsating, so I clicked them over and over. It was as if the computer had been spiritually hacked, leaving me with no control over it anymore. Even when I would power it down and restart it, the computer would inexplicably end up on odd websites. I was led to read strange and seemingly random articles. The selection made no sense to me on the rational level, but reading the articles tweaked a level of knowing that lay dormant somewhere in my cellular structure. I would also be asked to print pages of specific information about Mayan culture and told to keep them in a file for future reference.

One night, the intensity of the electronic waves—a cacophony of beeping and squeaking sounds in my ears related to strange frequencies—finally reached a fever pitch that I could no longer tolerate. I sensed adjustments were being made by my spiritual guides to regulate the energy flowing through me, but it wasn't working. I could no longer bear one more decibel of sound energy flowing through me. I picked up my laptop and walked outside to the swimming pool, where I paused only for a moment before throwing it into the water and watching it slowly sink to the bottom.

Next came the monitor and the speakers, and soon after that every television I could carry, along with digital clocks and any other device with electronic components. All were soon floating or lying at the bottom of my pool.

The only electronic things left in my house by morning were the built-in microwave oven and my large flat-screen TV. Had those things not been too heavy to lift, they too would have been in the pool. It had been quite a night.

The next morning, I woke up and walked out on the patio where I found Edgardo cleaning the pool. We were both silent as we stared at my collection of drowned electronics. When I told him to throw everything away, Maria and Carmen regarded me with disbelief and concern. The look on their faces at seeing the monumental waste of thousands of dollars' worth of equipment being piled into garden-sized trash bags told me I had lost my ability to reason. I could not understand how I could get to the point of such madness when there were so many people around me in need.

I began sobbing at what had become of me. I feared my inability to cope. Other than Deborah, who could possibly understand me? Even my faithful staff Carmen and Maria were staring at me with shame and pity, feeling useless at not knowing what to do or how to support me. Maria had always been my rock. She had worked hard all her life to break the cycle of poverty for her children. I did my best to support her in reaching for goals beyond those her culture had spelled out for her. Yes, she worked for me, but there was also a special bond between us. I had counted on her to have my back through so many ups and downs over the years, but there had never been anything like this.

I tried to explain the voices, sounds, and signals that were playing havoc with my mind. In her quiet wisdom, Maria simply said, "Senora, I think you should leave this place. There have been too many crazy things happening to you, and we are afraid for you."

She was right, too much of the unexplained was happening and I was spinning out of control. The only way to survive was to leave the lake—but go where? Considering the state I was in, where could I possibly go?

Because I questioned my sanity, I persuaded myself that there was no one in my intimate circles who could understand my circumstances. Outside of Deborah, who was going to believe all the crazy things that had happened? My family definitely wouldn't.

Yet, wait! There might be someone. I finally risked a call to my friend Bebe in Texas, who I prayed would understand. We had often talked about spiritual things and she seemed open to all the possibilities. I called Bebe and gave her the "light version" of what was happening, telling her that I needed to leave the lake immediately. My hope was that she could travel with me to Scottsdale where I planned to seek professional help.

Bebe and her husband were listening to me on Skype as I tried to find the words to convince them that I could not be alone. After hearing my stories of the many bizarre things that were happening to me, I knew they had their doubts. As they tried to put the pieces together from my scattered explanation, I could sense their confusion. I hung up the phone and hoped Bebe would meet me in Houston when I was between flights.

Later Bebe told me that after we hung up they were discussing the weird events I had described and whether Bebe should drop everything and meet me. They freaked out when her computer started randomly dinging and banging, and started realizing that what I was saying might have some merit. That led Bebe to pack her bags immediately and drive the three hours from San Antonio to meet me at the Houston airport just in time to make my connection to Phoenix.

Soon we were at a Scottsdale resort where I hoped to rest. After checking in, I began telling her the whole story of what happened. With Bebe, I was fortunately able to communicate in a more or less coherent fashion. Much to my surprise, Bebe knew a lot about the ancient Mayan culture, including their prophecies for 2012. She had read numerous books on the subject of the Mayan calendar, so her insight helped a great deal. We searched the internet to see if there were others who had got Mayan messages hoping to validate the many things that were happening to me.

I suggested that we go to the Mayo Clinic, as they had done a pretty good job fixing Tino. Bebe, however, was not at all on board with the idea that the Mayo Clinic could find a diagnosis for this otherworldly Mayan cocktail of unexplained events. Although I was convinced they could help, Bebe finally won out and we abandoned the idea of seeking mainstream professional help. She knew that I would probably be diagnosed with a mental illness that would lead to being institutionalized.

Bebe and I spent a week together organizing my thoughts. During that time, the sound of the voices in my head subsided and I did my best to put the whole affair behind me. For her part, Bebe did her best to ground me, trying to get me to come back to reality. After some intense work, our efforts seemed to have succeeded. At that point, she decided I would be okay and went home. I went on to California to my friend Cami's birthday party in Napa Valley.

On arrival at the house Cami rented, the spiritual voices and vibrations returned in full force. They had followed me. By the end of the first day, I was on my knees, this time begging God for answers and comfort, as I knew I could not sustain another round of spirits talking to me.

I canceled my participation in the next day's activities with my friends to be alone. After they left the house, the voices told me to pull my chair over to the bedroom window, open it, and then wait. By this time, I had become a rather obedient soul to the process, since I knew that whatever was going to occur could not be deterred. The spirit voices then told me to take a picture outside the window with my camera, and there in the viewfinder I saw a very soft beam of light! I took another picture, and there was a beautiful cross of light forming! I kept taking pictures in sequence, as this very soft, yet powerful energy started moving into my room. It came closer and closer as the angelic music my spirit guides had told me to download was playing on my iPod.

No words exist to describe the beauty of the feeling in my room. They continued to tell me that I had some kind of destiny with the planet Venus. The songs were all chanting about the goddess in me and the Milky Way.

I became limp and weak, as the energy that had been snapping and firing inside of me subsided. A globe of light that formed at the intersection of the two beams of the cross started to come closer and closer, heading for my heart until, like a blast, it entered me and I left my body.

In my "other" awareness I was flying around the house. I went to the gardens and hovered around the trees, looking down to the roof. I "floated" over to a patio table and sat, feeling I was dead. I waited, hoping that something would validate the change of my existence, and then I grew angry with Tino since he had not shown up when I was obviously on the other side. When I did not see him, I figured I must still be alive and I headed for the kitchen again for my usual validation. I could see the housekeeper, but she could not see me! I started dancing around her, throwing my arms in the air, and she did not react. I then picked up a pan and dropped it on the floor to see if she would hear the noise, but there was not even a blink from her. Really it was only my vision of a pan that I had thrown.

I was furious and frustrated. I was dead, but I was still here—so where was I? I "floated" again toward my bedroom, and when I saw my body lying there, I popped back into it.

Dazed and confused, I called Deborah. I rattled off an hour or so of untethered thoughts. She was a good listener, but she knew I was spinning out of control. After two out-of-body experiences it was getting harder and harder for me to get back to my original reality. I asked about Tino and she said he was fine, yet worried about me. She did not want to open any more doors to the spirit world until I did some grounding.

The weekend was coming to an end. At times I was fine, but other times I could not gather the pieces of myself together in some form of coherence. My thoughts were in total chaos, and this time the reality that I used to relate to others had vanished. In order to save face with my friends, I made an excuse to leave the birthday gathering and checked into a hotel near the airport in San Francisco.

I stayed in my room for two days, as it felt safer to be isolated. I was afraid to go back to El Salvador and face the continued unraveling of my mind, but I had to go somewhere. I went to the airport, still undecided as to where to go next, and decided that I would check into a spa that was in Ojai, California.

In the Los Angeles airport, I went to the rental car counter where the agent offered me a gratis upgrade to an Infinity sedan. This seemed rather odd because I did not have any special points or club membership. I went ahead and took the car. I drove north and decided to spend a few days at a spa and hope for the best. It felt right that I would be out of the vibrations of a city and nearer to nature.

Sitting on the balcony of my room under the shade of a beautiful oak tree, my energy was still in manifestation mode when three raccoons appeared on a tree branch that hung over my chair. I had a chat with them about their life at the spa. I looked at their little masked faces, wondering if they were spies, but most of all wondering how I could hear them speaking to me in the first place!

I called Bebe. She did her best to walk me back to normal, but even so I remained a fragmented mess. With only Bebe and Deborah left in my world as lifelines, the rope was getting thin. During the night, I spun out of control. I clenched my hair in my hands begging the voices to stop. I was seeing hundreds of faces of Mayan people in my mind.

In the morning, I checked out, got in my rental car, and headed for the coast of California. My intent was to kill myself. I parked on a cliff and started to write my last will and testament. I wanted to be sure my granddaughter with cerebral palsy would be okay, and that Bebe, who loved my cats, would take care of them until they passed on. I knew my staff at the lake would take care of the dogs in El Salvador.

I decided to put the paper in a safe place where someone would find it in case the crash scene had too much damage to recover it, so I got out of the car and placed my will securely under a rock near the cliff I would be driving off.

I started to cry—almost in relief—as I stared at the gear in the PARK position, knowing that as soon as it went to DRIVE I would be gone. I really didn't care about death as already I had been in and out of my body probably more times than I was aware of and the process was beginning to seem rather seamless. Yet this time I was in control of the process with the gearstick in my hand. I looked back on my life and felt I had done all I could to help others through my generosity, but when it had come to helping myself get back to Earth I did not have so much as a remote idea what to do. Most of all, I knew I could not reside in my body anymore. It was chaos with no way to flip a switch and turn it off. I was ready to call it quits.

I grabbed the gearstick to move it into DRIVE, but it would not go into any position except REVERSE, so I put it in PARK again. I tried again to move the gear-stick into DRIVE—no luck. At that moment, a voice came through the GPS system and commanded, "Today it is not your time. Go home." My head fell on the steering wheel in deep exhaustion as I realized I had to go on. I did not see how I was going to survive the way I was and with a sense of defeat, I backed up the car and got back on Highway 1.

Since I knew the flight to El Salvador departed at midnight, I still had some time to kill (no pun intended) so I keyed "closest Starbucks" into the car's GPS and was on my way. I followed the directions exactly, which led me to a random neighborhood nowhere near a Starbucks. I keyed in another Starbucks and yet again ended up nowhere near one. In one last effort, I followed the instructions to another Starbucks and found myself at Toys "R" Us. The car obviously had an agenda.

I pulled into a parking space and started to laugh. I laughed and laughed and looked around to see if I was in some kind of Hollywood joke's-on-me show, but no one showed up. Here I was, one moment ready to commit suicide and the next moment cracking up in the parking lot of Toys "R" Us.

I turned off the GPS and set out to find a Starbucks the old-fashioned way, by just driving around. I found one, ordered a latte, and plopped down on a couch. As I looked at the people around me going about their daily routines, I knew I was masquerading as a normal person.

I opened my brand-new computer (one I had purchased after the other one ended up in my pool), and it was completely whacked out. It flashed and seized up. I was unable to create new passwords and eventually I could not enter anything at all. I drove to an Apple store and after fourteen people scratched their heads, they gave me another new computer while the "old one" was on its way to Cupertino, California, for a full psychic evaluation.

I took the midnight flight home. I stared out the plane window into the darkness. As we were over the Pacific Ocean, the sky opened up and I saw two golden eyes staring at me. When they blinked, I realized they were the eyes of a jaguar. Startled, I looked around the plane to see if anyone else had noticed the eyes, but quickly gave up on that idea. A soft and tender energy then came over me, reminding me of the presence of jaguars now in my journey and the feeling of a deep sense of calm when they were there.

With the presence of this flying jaguar all the voices of spirits stopped and there was silence for the first time in a month.

My thoughts went out to Tino and how much I needed him, but for now he was silent. I learned later that he was afraid for me and did not want to add to my confusion of voices.

I arrived in the early hours of the morning at the El Salvador airport where Mario was again waiting for me. Back on the dirt road to the lake, the car crept through arches of lush green vines. Nearing home, I had the sense that things were closing in on me again. I faced being alone with the spiritual energies that had forced me to leave. There was no one I knew in El Salvador who I thought could possibly get their arms around the story of what was happening so I chose silence. I would remain alone with my thoughts, and my thoughts were mine alone.

The colors of the world around me that had been so vibrant before were now just dreary green blobs. I could no longer see the twinkling energy in things that had seemed so vivid. I arrived with no feeling of hope or belonging. The only blessing was seeing the dogs, Baco and Bruno, my three cats, and my household staff.

As I walked into the house, I remembered all the times I had brought Tino home after visiting a hospital in the United States. I felt Tino was lucky both before and after he left. He had me around all the time to manage his ups and downs and take care of his wounds. I, on the other hand, had only myself to take care of the broken-down mess of thoughts and voices that were plaguing me. It was me now who needed wound care.

CHAPTER FOURTEEN

IT SEEMED I WAS always a step away from the extraordinary. Back home, I was determined to do my best to be ordinary again. After unpacking, I told Maria to bring me a plate of beans and rice with a warm tortilla—my absolute favorite meal in the world. I needed nourishment and grounding, and the taste of the food was beyond amazing. The textures, the temperatures, the popping of flavors, and the sensory experience of all things, including food, was so welcome. Never had food tasted like that before. I snuggled up with my three cats on the bed and slept until the next morning.

I was experiencing so much of the unbelievable that my brain could not process it. Over and over the impossible became possible. My existing belief systems were being rapidly destroyed, and my reality was undergoing revision after incredible revision. Nothing added up any more, and as much as I was doing my best to sweep the multitude of thoughts and emotions into the dustpan, they would simply fly around in my head nevertheless so I could never get to a tidy place of understanding.

Whatever plan the spirits had for me was in full swing. After breakfast one day, I went to my office, anxious to get my third computer in as many months up and running, and to catch up on all of my personal affairs. Since I had ignored everything and abandoned communication with everyone for so long, I planned to begin making contact again. I spent most of the day on my computer, even though at times it was acting dysfunctional.

The ultimate trauma came when I had my bank account up on the screen and the cursor on my computer began moving without my hand on the mouse. I rebooted the computer, but when it was back up the cursor started moving on its own again. This time it went to my bank's website, typed in a password, and my bank account appeared. As I stared at my personal information, the screen flickered and the computer went totally dead.

In a panic, I started the computer again, my email inbox popped up, and I clicked on it. A threatening email stated that if I did not wire funds from my bank account into a specified account, I would be killed or kidnapped that afternoon. This was not the first time I had faced extortion in El Salvador, and it triggered all of the fears that I had been storing since the day I had moved there. This would be the final straw. I had been a tough cookie living there even though I had experienced a lot of violence, death, and injustice, but now I was falling deep into a spiral of trauma that I could not run from any more.

I reflected back on all the things that I had stuffed into the recesses of my mind, and as soon as I opened the door, everything I had suppressed came tumbling out. A movie reel of traumas commenced: the crash in a hot air balloon, being thrown out of a fishing boat and almost drowning, being hit by a freak wave and crashing into rocks that cut me like razor blades, an ambush by communist guerrillas with AK-47s, a bomb that blew up near me while I was getting into my car, helicopters with bullet casings cascading on my roof, seeing dead bodies scattered in the street when I opened my garage door, a drive-by shooting outside of my restaurant, harassment from a perverted stalker, Tino's passing, and now having my computer hacked by blackmailers. All of it came blasting out of my mind. I felt like I had been broken open, like a *piñata,* and all of my very hidden and dramatic traumas had spilled out and were now scattered on the floor.

The last of my fight-or-flight hormones came pouring out of my adrenal glands, magnifying my responses beyond belief. I told Maria about the message and she and I immediately packed a carryon. I jumped into my car and drove to the airport so I could get out of the country. I bought a ticket to Houston and three hours later was in the customs area of the Houston airport. It was midnight. I had called Bebe from the El Salvador departure lounge, asking if I could stay with her in San Antonio, and she did not fail me. I rented a car and drove down a dark Texas highway, reaching her home around 3:00 A.M. Through this entire muddle, her voice and Deborah's were the only ones I trusted.

The sun was rising as we sat in Bebe's office with much-needed coffee and debated the same question: What next? First, I changed all the passwords on my accounts and managed to hold off a frontal assault on my private information. Then, the conversation turned to what was happening to me. I asked her please to help me find a way out of the situation in which I now found myself. For several hours, we Googled long-tail keyword phrases, such as *hearing uncontrollable voices, Mayan ancestors, light beams, out-of-body experiences,* and anything else we could think of, to find anyone with a specialty in these phenomena or who had reported a similar experience as mine. There was no one. We even discussed the possibility of me going to a psychiatrist again, but agreed it was not an option.

Bebe said that during the last month she and Deborah had been talking almost daily. Deborah was working, from the spiritual side, on what was going on with me. Bebe had shared all of our conversations with her and was keeping a lifeline to me by calling me every day. We called Deborah who was always standing by to help. She suggested I contact a very talented shaman named Marilyn who had miraculous gifts that she had inherited from her mystical grandmother, who came from Haiti. Unfortunately, Marilyn was out of town.

I needed help right away.

I really could not live alone anymore as my head space was filled with a stew of spiritual voices mixed with past traumas, and with all that had happened in the past few months, Bebe and I came to the conclusion that my mind was now fragmented beyond normal methods of repair.

Bebe then recalled a friend who had been in a mental hospital for almost two years in Peru, suffering from severe mental depression. Bebe called the friend, explained my symptoms to her, and her friend agreed that going to a conventional psychiatrist would get me tossed into a mental ward and put on massive doses of drugs that very afternoon, just as had happened to her. The woman, however, knew of a young shaman and spiritual worker in Colombia whom she believed would be able to assist me with my troubles. The shaman, a man named Oscar, had done amazing work with her, and in fact, got her released from the mental hospital, because her real problem was not mental, but spiritual in nature. As the friend spoke of Oscar's ability, she encouraged us to call him immediately for his evaluation of my situation.

The next day Bebe called Oscar. He quickly tapped into my energy remotely and told her I was living in a state of chaos. Spirits with good and bad energy were entering and leaving my body, my mind, and my spirit. He also said I was being bombarded by information that often was not in my best interest. Oscar had perfectly described what was going on, without Bebe or I sharing a tidbit of my symptoms or experiences.

Oscar said he would do his best by "cleaning" me up by sending me long-distance healing energy from Colombia and prescribing me an exotic blend of potions that I would prepare. I did my best to translate everything he said into English and then searched for the items on his list on the internet and had them shipped to me overnight. Oscar had given me a shopping list for camphor, mugwort, Florida water, eggs, oregano, ammonia, garlic, white sage, and mothballs. Under his instruction, my room quickly filled with the aromas of sage and sandalwood. In addition, he asked that three times a day I get down on my knees in Bebe's guesthouse and read verses from the Bible over and over.

Oscar continued to call with new lists of ingredients for potions. Afterward he would spend time in trance trying to find the magical combination to clear me. Before bed I left cut lemons in corners, I smudged the room with smoking cedar bundles and sticks of palo santo, and drank special herbal teas. My dreams became lucid and full of visions, to the point that the line between my dream state and my waking state was blurring. There were times the only way I could discern if I was truly awake was that my eyes were open.

After a couple of weeks of long-distance healing it was decided that the situation was much more difficult to resolve than Oscar had anticipated. He told me that my only option was to work with him and other shamans directly by traveling to Colombia. Although I feared going into Colombian jungles alone, at least I spoke Spanish. Truly I had reached the point where I would go anywhere and do anything to win back my peace of mind. Without some kind of intervention, I was afraid that I would not survive—or that I would end up being confined to an institution for the rest of my life.

Bebe and I had no doubt that my issues had spiritual implications, and even though we kept revisiting mainstream psychiatry as a solution, we finally admitted there were few options left. My greatest relief was that Bebe believed I was truly experiencing everything I shared with her and so I trusted her. In my last threads of desperation, I decided to brave the Colombian jungles and seek help from Oscar the shaman.

The night before leaving, I tossed and turned with thoughts of going to Colombia. Sensing my vulnerability, before I left the next morning Bebe took me into her mother's bedroom and opened a wooden box containing a rose quartz rosary. Placing it around my neck, she told me to go find my peace—that it existed somewhere inside of me and I should never forget that. I headed for Houston and my flight to Colombia.

CHAPTER FIFTEEN

I N Bogota, I caught a prop plane to the jungle. I arrived late in the afternoon at a small, bustling city near
a river. I waited outside the airport, which was no bigger
than a Starbucks. Drenched from heat and humidity, I felt
and looked awful, as all my energy had been consumed in
the sheer journey of just getting there. Besides, I was on the
verge of a complete breakdown of all my mental and emotional resources.

Finally, Oscar arrived. He was a thin young man with
large brown eyes and a flashing ivory smile. He gave me
a hug then placed his hands on his hips as he studied me,
squinting his eyes as if to see what was inside. He had a
take-charge personality, as if he had all the reassurance in
the world that things would be all right.

Oscar, his brother, Nico, and I piled into a mini taxi
and headed for Oscar's house. Passing through dilapidated
neighborhoods, I reminded myself not to hold any expectations of what I might find on this journey. "Go with an
open mind, be willing to receive the work, and don't judge,

no matter what initial impressions you might have," I kept mumbling under my breath.

Bumping along the dirt streets, I was coming to the realization that this trip to the underbelly of the world of mystics and magic would not be an easy one. To survive it, I would need to find my point of surrender and humble myself to receive whatever I needed to get better. I would be putting my life in the hands of people I did not know and be forced to accept the power of things that I could not see before.

The taxi stopped in front of a small storefront with glass cases full of colorful potions. There were products to generate positive results for finances, careers, and relationships. There were also potions designed to ward off evil spirits and cleanse people from spiritual intrusions. There were plaster statues of revered spirit helpers I would soon come to know: Negro Felipe, a former slave; India Rosa (the namesake of the store), a sexy Indian woman who loved perfume and cigarettes; and Guaicaipuro, an Indian man who had viciously fought off Spanish invaders in the fifteenth century and liked drinking *guaro* ("firewater") and smoking cigars.

At the center of them all was Maria Lionza, a beautiful spirit who carried an almost angelic feeling about her. She lived in the mountains and the indigenous people of Colombia attributed to her many of the same characteristics of love, beauty, sex, and fertility, similar to the goddess Venus.

There was also Don Juan del Dinero, a former banker who helped with matters of money, and another spirit who was a benefactor to small children.

All these spirits had once been living people.

Symbols from all the world's religions hung on the walls of the shop, with an emphasis on Catholic angels and saints.

Oscar was very proud to show me his newest acquisition, a figurine of a beautiful Hindu goddess sitting cross-legged with a large blue ball on her lap. She was painted gold and had plastic stones in her headdress. Next to her was a figure of the archangel Gabriel, caught in the act of slaying an evil spirit who was being crushed under his foot. I especially related to this one. Large candles in the shapes of pyramids stood tall above the multitude of objects, all with their own dose of spiritual value. There seemed to be a mixture of religion and indigenous "cures" for everything, as well as a steady stream of customers coming to Oscar for spiritual readings and the appropriate potions to solve their problems. I walked through the little store in awe that all of this even existed and marveling at the confidence his clientele had in the products and divinations Oscar would give them.

After saying my hellos to the rest of his family and Oscar shooing away the line of people still interested in shamanic readings, my new shaman friend gathered up a big box of herb potions and candles from the store and we hopped into another taxi. We were going to see Farides, the woman at whose home my rituals of cleansing would take place. She was Oscar's mentor and the town's most respected shaman. Because of the sweltering heat, plastic fans from China were a hot item in the storefronts, blowing strings of colored ribbons and offering bargain prices with monthly payments. There was no sign of affluence anywhere, only the hum of daily survival. We passed colorful neighborhoods with hot pink houses and homemade speed bumps, finally arriving at a simple brown house that had not seen a fresh paint job for too many years.

We entered Farides's house, where several people were waiting for us. Oscar introduced them to me as *brujos* and *brujas,* which in English means "male witches" and "female witches." That brought a big, scary question to mind: *Am I consorting with witches?* Soon I learned that in this part of the world the term *witch* was used to describe all indigenous healers. There was a tacit understanding that Oscar's group of brujos were for positive work, as opposed to others who specialized in malevolence. It was also apparent that these spiritual workers knew a lot about the dark side of things and were like bulldozers dedicated to clearing all spiritual adversity that they found along their way.

A brujo who had been waiting for us jumped up and dragged over a plastic chair so I could sit under a tree on the back patio where we would do our work. The patio held old tires, plastic water containers, an old wheelbarrow, and pieces of discarded rebar. As I captured the scene, I felt a strong energy and knew this was a place where many other rituals had been held. There was a calm-before-the-storm feeling.

I waited while Oscar gave orders to the other brujos. As he did, a white cat with one green eye and one blue eye came near me, adding more mystery to the scene. Some of the kids who were playing in the house snuck a peek at me, the *gringa* who had come from the United States.

Oscar was always "on" and had no patience for anyone or anything except his work. He was determined to fix me, and I could tell he was listening to the spirits in his head, as he always seemed distracted and did not interact much with anyone. I also sensed the other brujos were listening to spirits, since I had become very familiar with what that felt like and looked like from my own experience. The flurry of our arrival had subsided and we were all seated and waiting for Farides to appear.

A dirt circle had been left open in the cement patio, and I assumed this was where ceremonial fires took place. Two more brujos arrived. I said hello and they acknowledged me as they casually pulled out several rolled cigars. They covered their heads with handkerchiefs, and sat near me until finally Farides appeared in the doorway. A large woman dressed in turquoise capris pants, a pink tee-shirt, and rubber flip-flops, she shuffled toward the circle. She also wore a handkerchief on her head. Her salt and pepper hair was in a short, no-nonsense haircut, and she smiled at me as she drew closer.

Farides carried a brown bag full of hand-rolled cigars, which she dropped near the circle's edge. She had a special chair, which was plastic like mine, but with the legs cut off to a height that kept her face to face with the fire. She took out five cigars and began moving them between her fingers, then tapping them so they lined up straight in the palm of her hand.

Oscar took his place beside her with his own set of cigars. No questions. No conversation. Just a hopeful glance at me, and we were ready to begin.

I had gotten the scoop on Farides and Oscar's relationship before I had arrived. Her fifty-five years gave her a level of prestige and authority above all the others. Having seen the potential of Oscar's spiritual powers when he was a child, she had taken him on as her protégé. I could tell that Farides admired Oscar's gift much more than she did any of the others in the group.

Black and white candles were pulled from the bag we had brought, and Farides pulled a pen from behind her ear. Both my name and the date of my birth were written on each candle, which were then placed in the sign of a cross. The candles were lit and the ceremony began.

Oscar started chanting and I could tell he was calling in the spirits. I recognized some of the names he was calling out to from the plaster statues I had seen at the store. All the brujas began lighting up their cigars and connecting with the spiritual world. I was told to sit with my arms open and repeat a mantra of my intentions for healing. "I am ready to receive whatever it is I am about to receive for my highest good and the highest good of others." I asked Jesus and God to be with me and to help the brujos heal me and give me back my peace of mind.

I would later see some of the pictures they had taken of me at the ceremony, and there was nothing near a smile on my face. My mouth was stuck in drenched surrender. I did not have a muscle left in my face to force a smile; since by the time the ceremony began I was void of all emotion. I had reached this moment with the last ounce of effort I had, and when the ceremony started I surrendered the entire process to whatever power would come and give me back my life—or take it—it didn't matter.

The intention of the first session was to rid me of all the bad spirits around me, so the brujos tried to entice them into the candles' flames. They began smoking five and six cigars at a time in order to communicate with the spirits. The success and failure could be determined by watching the color of the ashes and how the smoke reacted. It seemed that everything was hinging on what the ashes would do. All the answers were in the ashes. Did the ashes fall? Did they turn white? Black? Did they continue in long streams and stay fixed and firm on the cigar, or did they crumble and fall off instantly? I would learn that if they turned a golden color we were making progress.

The brujas remained fixated on the cigars and talked among themselves about the conclusions they were drawing from the smoking, until they reached a consensus and came up with some answers that I hardly understood. At the end of the ceremony, after enticing bad energies into the fire, the candles exploded and supposedly any spirits that had decided to latch on to me were eliminated. It was a long evening. I had been there over five hours and Oscar could see I needed to stop. He took me back to the hotel room they had chosen for me, which was up three stories and all the way in the back of the building, overlooking an alley and the river.

Oscar stayed a while with me in my little room, yet he did not share any details about the process. I guess it was futile to try to explain the unseen world to a rookie like me. He did, however, get right to the point and stated there would be a minimum of ten rituals needed to ensure a complete purification process. He opened the door to a bathroom—which I was grateful to see was inside my room—and placed four cloves of garlic in a glass of water, which he then put under my bed. He told me that when the four cloves were floating on top of the glass I would be cured and could go home. He wished me sweet dreams with a skeptical look and said his brother would be there in the morning to take me to the next session.

I took out a picture of Tino I had brought with me. At that moment I had never felt so alone and so vulnerable. There was no concierge to be found and no internet to even find myself on a Google map. I opened the small window and salsa music came barging through, as well as the sound of frantic cars passing by. Sounds were still amplified in my ears, impossible to turn down.

I placed the picture of Tino on the pillow beside me as I went to bed. I asked him over and over how I had ever gotten to this place. What had gone wrong, and why was I paying such a high price? Although I was afraid even to listen to the voices of spirits, I did feel Tino's frustration. He seemed as confused as I was, although I sensed he, in some way, was supporting me. I also realized I was in deep spiritual trouble.

CHAPTER SIXTEEN

THE NEXT MORNING, I was digging into the week's supply of granola bars I had brought to Colombia and trying to make a cup of coffee in a French press using tepid water from the bathroom faucet. Before I'd left the ritual the previous night, one of the brujos, Carmen, confessed to me that I was the hardest case they had ever encountered. Most people like me never even got to them. Either they took their own lives or got locked up in mental institutions. Her candid remarks had me realize the seriousness of what was happening. I wondered about the very few who had come before me. I vowed to do everything they told me. I had to, since I had no place left to turn.

Oscar rarely was awake before noon as he spent the nights in cemeteries rallying dislocated spirits to help in the effort. So every day after lunch we would meet on Farides' patio. Different brujos would come and go, helping to do the work of smoking the cigars, but I could sense Oscar was the rock star among them. Everyone around Oscar marveled at how he orchestrated the spiritual world. He could summon spirits and integrate them within himself, something no one else in the community was capable of doing. These were very powerful spirits who had the capacity for resolution of the bigger issues.

As the brujos smoked their cigars, we would all sit around the candles, watching them explode with a popping sound and begin to melt. Peering into the fire created by the melted candles, I could see malevolent-looking faces arising within the flames. There was a feeling of relief as the harmful spirits whose faces these were flew up and disintegrated into the night sky. I did not entirely understand what was going on. But the brujos around me, who were normally tough cookies, seemed to be in awe of the number of spirits that were being extracted through this process. They indicated that my personal energy field was being cleansed.

After sitting in smoke for hours, I felt I was being hollowed out—that the brujos were emptying me of whatever was dominating me. Farides told me my body had been compromised almost beyond repair and said I should be grateful to have my mind back in some kind of functioning state. She also continued to remind me about two other women she had tried her best to clear who had both eventually ended up in mental institutions. This generated many questions, but I was fighting for my life and my sanity, so I was not going to waste time figuring it out. I wanted to be back in life again, whole and capable of functioning. The ceremonies would last late into the night. Then, after dropping me off at my hotel, Oscar would head out into the darkness, still on the case.

The fourth night involved a larger ceremony. Fifteen brujos came, as it seemed they had decided that they were going to make a full force effort toward my healing. I was given a white gauze dress and told to stand in the center of their circle, then to close my eyes. I do not know what they did, but I soon felt smoke and the swirling of energy around me. There was chanting and singing and I felt many spirits there. I kept repeating my mantra and the Bible verses, asking the Mayan spirits I had come in contact with at the lake to come and aid in my protection. Also I continued to call for the four jaguars that were my protectors.

All of a sudden, the scene shifted. I opened my eyes to see Oscar breathing deeply and moving around in strange contortions. As I watched with disbelief and confusion, I was reassured that he was all right, and that one of the spirits was entering his body. This seemed to be totally unexpected and the brujos were scrambling around to get enough money to go next door to a liquor store and buy guaro. In the meantime, they were able to find a bottle with a small amount left. Carmen excitedly said, "Lori, I think this spirit is coming into Oscar's body to talk to you." The spirit then incorporated itself into Oscar as everyone scrambled for a chair. Oscar sat down next to a small table with the guaro, as well as some rolled cigars, on it. I was sitting directly in front of Oscar's body, but the Oscar I knew was gone.

Honestly, I do not remember being afraid. I had been through so much by this time that I was willing to accept everything that went on there. I could feel the spirit inside Oscar and was told it was the spirit of Guaicaipuro. As I sat in front of him, Oscar's mouth opened and the voice of a boisterous Indian came through. He knew my name and why I had come there. All the brujos seemed to be very surprised at this and they gathered around so as not to miss a word. The Indian told me that his brothers, my friends the Mayans, were there and were helping me. He pointed behind me at them. I had also felt the presence of Mayan spirits and was surprised to hear this confirmed. They told Guaicaipuro that they were the ones who brought me the butterflies and dragonflies at the lake. I smiled since no one else there knew of that miraculous private moment.

The Indian then had a stern complaint about my lack of reverence for the spirits who were helping me, as I was not sufficiently thankful for all the work they were doing. He also complained about my ignorance of the process and my lack of belief in the brujos' ability to cure me. He was right. Deep in my subconscious I had been dragging my doubts through the entire process, and I believe this was causing frustration in the way these people and the spirits were able to affect their work.

I have since learned that intention is the key to spiritual healing, and I was being exposed for doubting many of the things the brujos were doing. He was angry and told me that I would fail if I did not believe in them. The Indian also said that I was lucky to have such powerful Mayan spirits come to free me from the torture I was experiencing. He then asked for the bottle of liquor and started drinking, smoking, and voicing his opinions about the work of other brujos and things they were doing that were not helping either. Then he told Farides that I needed to help clean up her altar.

With that, the Indian finished the last gulp of guaro. When he asked for more, it had not yet been brought home from the liquor store so he gave everybody a tongue lashing. It was a tense moment as the Indian ranted about what a pain it was to incorporate into human bodies and not find a sufficient supply of his favorite bottle of liquor waiting for him. Guaicaipuro then left and, after ten minutes of bodily contortions, Oscar was back in control of his body. The ceremony was abruptly over. They called a taxi and, with a quiet Oscar in the back seat, I was taken to my hotel.

The next day, the same routine of smoking cigars and blowing up candles, and chanting ensued, but this time I was taken to an area near the altar that had a wall around it. Behind the wall, I noticed several buckets of water. I was told to stand there in the dark and close my eyes. I could hear Oscar and Farides opening bottles of potions and pouring them into the different buckets. Then they were lifting the buckets over my head and drenching my body. Each bucket had a different smell. Some were sweet and fragrant, others pungently strong. The potions seemed to run deep into every vein and bone in my body.

I was then left alone to bathe with coarse soaps, the residue of which I was told to leave on my body. I finally dressed and was taken back to my hotel. Only later would I learn that even after I had gone back to the hotel, Oscar and Farides continued to work late into the night.

The following day Nico, Oscar's brother, picked me up in the taxi and we tried to get to Oscar's house, but traffic was terrible. Every turn presented another problem. What would normally be a ten-minute ride was now almost an hour, and I felt the positive energy slipping away. A fear that something was going very wrong came over me and I was growing desperate to get to Oscar. We finally got out of the taxi and walked the remaining distance, only to find him yelling at me, telling me the situation was still volatile and now I was late.

Although I told him I felt the energies keeping me from getting to him, Oscar said he was done with me. He felt I was not supporting him enough, so he was calling it quits. This seemed crazy since, I was even more committed to the cause after the scolding from the Indian. I had even spent most of the morning meditating all my doubts away. But Oscar told me to go back to the States because there was nothing more they could do for me. It was over. I just sat there in shock. Oscar's brother, Nico, was also in disbelief.

I insisted that we try to talk and work out whatever was bothering Oscar, but he stormed out of the house. I, however, was not going to let him give up on me, so I remained there—hoping and praying he would come back—which he did two hours later. He told me he had gone to talk to the spirits, and that they told him negative forces were trying to separate us. All the pushing back was coming from the energies we were fighting for my mental freedom. When Oscar realized it was a concerted attempt to destroy everything we had accomplished so far, he had decided to come back to get me and we returned to the patio.

He talked at length with Farides, as they seemed to be planning a different strategy, which would put me back at the fire. More buckets and buckets of water were prepared, with probably fifteen different bottles of potions standing by. More and more explosive candles came out, and they took my watch off and threw it into the water as they said it was being used to transmit negative energies into my body. My hair was washed with bitter, foul-smelling soap and there was smoke and more smoke from more cigars, and screaming and chanting, until I was saturated with smoke and potions over and over. They told me I was not to wash them off until the morning.

For the first time I felt something had shifted. As the water came smashing over my head over and over, I lost my ability to speak and gasped for words and air, yet nothing came. Oscar and Farides told me to stop trying to speak and just to shake my head in an affirmative motion if I was all right, which I did.

Finally, they stopped and covered me with towels. I was also handed a collection of white clothing borrowed from Farides, who told me that for the rest of my stay I could only wear white. I was ordered to throw away all of my other clothes, including most of what was in my suitcase back at the hotel.

I arrived back to the hotel, grabbed most of the dark clothing I had and tossed it into a dumpster outside. Then I went to my room and got on my knees in gratitude for everyone who had come to help me that night. After the Indian's scolding I had realized the importance of having faith and feeling gratitude for everything and everyone. I felt we had turned a corner, experiencing a huge release from the negative energy that was attached to me.

I reached for my small flashlight and kneeled down on the linoleum floor, shining the light on the glass Oscar had placed under my bed. I took a deep breath and saw that two cloves of garlic had floated to the surface! If I could have slept on my knees and sent out gratitude all night long I would have, but my body had reached its point of collapse. With my last ounce of energy, I finally crawled into the bed.

The next thing I knew it was morning, and I was still covered in the smell of all the potions penetrating my body. My hair looked like a mop, as locks of it had now formed clumps the size of dreadlocks due to the white, chalk-like substance covering them. I walked to the bathroom and looked in the mirror, at first taken aback by what I saw. I was completely white. I first thought there was a paste covering my skin, but I soon realized, after running my hand over my face several times, that it wasn't. It was the color of my skin.

I stared intently into my blue eyes and something was different. They seemed clearer, not the dismal gray they had become since this had all started. I sought a deeper view and was surprised that a little starlight peeked back out to me. The brujas had gone into my soul and opened it up to that speck of light, which glittered from my eyes! This was hope! This was a spark of life again!

The energies were much less chaotic on this day. When I arrived at Farides's house the kids playing in the living room motioned for me to go to her bedroom. Farides also seemed calmer and smiling, laying on her bed with a few of the brujas talking to her. She patted a spot near her and told me to sit down, assuring me that things were going well and to keep the faith. I told her I felt better, but it seemed as if my thoughts were still being observed and there were spirits still around me. As I was telling her this, a strong energy came blasting into my body, sending me straight up in the air. I came crashing down on the bed and Farides and all the brujas bounced up as I hit the mattress. We all looked at each other in amazement. The whole scene was so strange that they all started laughing. Farides, however, did not see the humor in it and told everyone to get out to the patio where there was work to do.

This day Oscar had not shown up and Farides took charge of the process. She sat on her special chair to begin the ceremony after telling her grandchildren, who were peeking at us from the back door, to go get her book. She then asked for quiet while flipping through the pages of her handwritten potions. I was fascinated with the different recipes she had written over the years. By this time, we had built up a level of confidence, so I felt comfortable asking her to show her recipes to me. She agreed and explained the different potions and spells. She also told me she was looking for something to clear my eyes so I would see only the light. I thought it was fascinating that she was focusing on the very thing that held my attention earlier that day.

Farides sent some of the brujas to buy herbs and told me to sit under the tree that had been shade for us during the day.

She told me I had a great power and that it was time for me to use it. I needed to remove all doubt and fight for my sanity and myself. She did not want me to use words of anger, but instead bring into myself the concept of power over everything. She said I was learning to be invisible to any external forces and to open my eyes and let the sun come into them.

I looked up into the tree and saw the eyes of spirits, and I knew these were not good spirits. It was as if they were the same ones extracted from me before, yet they were hanging around to see if I had room for them again. I stared into the eyes of these spirits and felt a weakness overcome me until Farides yelled at me to not get into an exchange. "Focus only on the sun! Focus only on the sun!" She kept me focusing on the entry of power from the sun and the tree to build up my resistance.

It was like a power standoff between my ability to infuse light and the negative energies' desire to return. My doubts, however, did not come in. I remained unwavering in my intention. The light kept building inside me and the spirits kept moving further and further away. At times I would slightly weaken and smoke would be blown into my eyes to protect me from losing ground. This went on for a while until Farides felt all the negative energies had dissipated.

While this was going on, the brujos kept smoking their cigars and watching the ashes to measure the progress, and when conditions were all-positive we felt that we had turned the corner.

I then waited until it was dark when Oscar finally showed up with more potions. He was very quiet, only telling me to prepare for more baths. He and Farides did not speak. I watched them working quietly and diligently and I felt they were preparing something very significant. I went back to the shower area where they waited and I took off my clothes. Without any notice they picked up two large buckets and drenched me with water. I screamed and shuddered, as it was the most cold and piercing bath I had so far received. I yelled at Oscar with some not so kind words in Spanish and asked him to tell me what he had thrown all over me, but the two of them just stared at me, then threw me a towel as they turned and walked away.

My body was in shock. I could hardly move. It was as if I had been thrown into frozen water, but the water wasn't cold. My breathing was short as I kept gasping for air and coughing. I could hear the soft voices of the brujos as they gathered their things to leave. There were no lights on other than the moon to light my space. I ran my hands over my body to see if it was still intact, and to verify that I was still physically present, as the shock waves from the bath continued to reverberate through my system. My insides were cold, but it was a good cold, as if I was left with a crystal inside me that was absolutely impenetrable.

My clothes were in a wet bundle on the cement floor and I tried to peel them apart to find some way to slither into them. Through the darkness I could see the altar and the plaster faces of all the spirits who were helping me. I was naked with a small towel around my waist and I walked to the altar, sending waves of gratitude to all the positive spirits. I looked into the night sky, celebrating the moon shining and the stars twinkling.

Back in my hotel I prayed that this was the final day. It had now been almost a week of nightly rituals and I was feeling that physically there was no more strength in me. I got down on my knees to peek under the bed. There I saw that the last clove of garlic was just below the surface! I lay on my back on the floor and felt I had made it–I was very close to going home!

Oscar showed up the next morning and wanted to see the garlic. He was also pleased, saying we would spend the day on the purification process. I was feeling that my body was slowly becoming crystalline—like my cells had been purged of all negativity and were lit up with energy—yet my physical body was still in shock and unable to function normally. I walked crookedly. I felt funny. My whole cellular structure was in a strange state of disconnection.

I was taken to a local shopping center and told to buy offerings for the different spirits who had helped me. I bought silk flowers, beautiful ribbons, vases, and plastic fruit. I found stars on sale as it was October and the Christmas decorations had already been put out.

Arriving at Oscar's house, I saw statues of each of the spirits we had been working with during my visit in a back bedroom with candles lit all around them. He told me I should start working on decorating and preparing an altar to honor them. I carefully wrapped the glittering ribbon around each item, then arranged roses and fruit in the knots. Each spirit required a different colored candle. Oscar had carefully explained this and I was careful not to make a mistake and upset him or them. I felt so much love for all of them and the deepest gratitude for their help to me. I talked to them, cried and laughed about the whole process, and felt an attachment that remains to this day.

Oscar came back an hour later to check on my progress, and then told me to lie on the painted cement floor as white candles were placed around me. He told me to stay there until all the candles burned to the ground. I was there for hours—just the candles, me, and the statues of the spirits.

As I lay there, there was time for reflection on what had happened. I realized the struggle included all of us together, fighting for my freedom. It was an amazing spiritual team of love and compassion fighting for a woman they hardly knew, a woman who showed up at the airport without hope. When I was lying among the candles, Oscar admitted that there were moments when he and Farides thought I was a lost cause. It was the most difficult clearing they had ever been involved in. He emphasized that it was a miracle that I survived this, and that the spirits had given me my life back. He was still cautious and concerned, saying there was the potential that I could be again under siege, but he felt certain the balance of power had significantly changed. I had a chance at life again.

I understood there were no guarantees in this business and that now I needed to be the shaman doing the work to protect myself.

After all the candles had burned to the ground, it was over. I wanted to go out to lunch and have a much-needed, nourishing meal. Oscar, Nico, and Nico's eight-year-old daughter, Nicole, hopped in a taxi with me and we headed for a restaurant. With both of them watching spirits around me, I asked them who the spirits were. "Don't worry, *Señora*," Oscar told me. "They are all good spirits—lots of Mayans, your jaguars, and some of our guys, too!"

That night I happily slept with my four floating garlic cloves under my bed. The next day I told Nico to take me to Farides, as I wanted to take offerings to her altar as well. When I arrived at her house, she took me to a corner of the patio and said it was time to talk. I knew she knew much more about me than she had let on.

Through the entire process she had never asked one question about me. She'd been focused on my survival until this moment. I asked her what she could tell me about how I got there and she wanted to know about the lake. I had never told her about Ilopango; she only knew I had come from

San Antonio recommended by a mutual friend of Oscar. When I told her about the lake incident, she just smiled and listened. She explained that I had been chosen. All I had gone through was an initiation into the spirit world. She assured me the Mayan spirits had been with me through the entire process, and admitted that when I arrived I was in big trouble, because she and Oscar at times thought they were in over their heads.

I asked her how it was possible that I had been so infested with so many dark energies? She shared that since I was hit by the beam of light I had become like a bright light bulb. Negative energies were like moths attracted to me. Since I had no frame of reference of how to protect myself I had become infested.

She told me that thanks to the powers I had around me and the strength of my mind, which was unwavering, I came through it all safely. She held my hands and sweetly squeezed them, saying, "Lori, you have the gift. You are to be greatly respected for this experience. Now you have been given all the tools to protect yourself. You have all the skills now as they live inside of you. We simply were the support you needed to get you to this place in your journey. You are a bruja or shaman, as you would say in the north. Just like many of us have learned, you need to find your power.

"Negative energies were trying to put you in a mental state that could get you institutionalized, a convenient place for isolating you and dimming your light, but your shamanic powers kept you safely on the path to serve others."

Farides left me with words of caution that who I was and what was housed in me could continue to bring me tests of faith and that I might need to call on the skill within me. She told me there were great forces in the lake which would support me. They would also have an impact on the people living in El Salvador.

"There is much compassion for those who are helping the spirits who live under the lake. The Mayans sent a great storm over the lake to clean the rivers and restructure the natural areas, just to impede access and stop development there. The lake is a sacred place. It is a portal of positive energy for the people of El Salvador. There is much to learn about the spiritual importance of the lake to the entire region."

I felt honored that Farides would speak to me like a colleague and that she had respect for what I had just endured. I had survived her rituals and never complained or denied what they were doing. I accepted everything they did. The entire time I had walked the path of the shaman, trusting the unknown, thus I came out on the other side, in the light.

Oscar was waiting in the doorway, watching us speak face to face while we were sharing our thoughts about what had happened. Eventually he told me to hurry up, as it was time to go to the airport. I embraced Farides and was never more grateful to a human being in my life. I left in tears at having to say goodbye.

At the airport, Oscar stood with both hands on my shoulders and said, "How come you never told me you had the gift when we first talked?" He looked at me with curiosity as if I had been keeping it a secret. Then he chuckled and teased me, saying, "You are a bruja."

I jokingly told him that I never knew it until I started hanging out with him and he smiled, telling me he felt honored to have been the one to heal me. I had a good laugh when he told me I was the first gringa who actually had the nerve to come see him in person. All of the work he had done in the past with those living in the United States was done long distance. He continued to caution me about his success rate, as these things were not well defined. But he said he felt I had all I needed to continue down a spiritual path. He said he wanted to come to the lake and do ceremonies with me there as he felt sure it was a remarkable place. We left this as a possibility for some day in the future.

Oscar's expression then grew somber. He had a warning for me, "Lori, I still see visions of you in a mental hospital. The spirits that we took on for you still have this as their goal. There is a karmic reason that they cannot kill you, but they can drive you to do it yourself. They do not want you walking about the world with the amount of light energy that you have, so their only option is to lock you up. You have a great destiny with the spirit world and there are those who do not want you to succeed at this important task. I am still troubled by this, and I want you to know this before you go home."

I thanked Oscar for taking care of me, then walked into the airport, turning back once more to see him waving at me with the sparkle of energy he always carried in his eyes. I stored his warning in my memory banks, and was ready to go home.

CHAPTER SEVENTEEN

IT WAS AN ALL-NIGHT flight from Colombia back to Houston. I tried to sort out everything that had happened, but realized it just needed to be left as it was. I had faced evil and death and learned that the only way to overcome evil was with goodness. Resisting evil did not work. From then on I would need to ignore forces that were not in my best interest by not giving up any of my powerful energy to things I did not want, and instead focusing exclusively on what I valued: my peace. The power the negative spirits had over me was only as deep as the fear I had of them and the doubt that I would succumb to that power. When I was not "against" anything, I found peace and calm.

I finally arrived back to Houston and drove to neighboring San Antonio, where Bebe was very relieved to see me in a much different state than when I left. I started to take responsibility for my life again, going back to my laptop and attending to normal things, such as paying bills and making decisions.

Since going back to the lake was not an option, I decided to move back into the small patio home I still owned in

Scottsdale. I needed a lot of "normal" and time to sort out my spiritual gifts. I had literally disappeared weeks earlier from El Salvador, and this had raised a lot of speculation from family and friends as to what was going on in my life. Yet, I was far from openly explaining to anyone what had happened to me. My story was unbelievable—even to me!

I could not bear being without my pets, so I had Baco and Bruno and my cats, Toe, Footsie, and Canela, flown to Houston. I spent a month with Bebe getting my thoughts, my strength, and some plans together for the future. Bebe and I then packed up the furry family and drove together to Arizona in an SUV I purchased. Bebe stayed with me for a few weeks, helping me get settled.

Bebe decided to go with me on my next adventure to Sedona. She was also going through a lot of her own life challenges, and I wanted our first day to be about her and not me, since it seemed that my issues had dominated matters for so many months.

Browsing in a Sedona shop, we found pamphlets advertising many psychics who were living in Sedona, and Bebe randomly chose one for a reading. We made a call and were soon knocking on the psychic's door.

This woman had years of experience and was well known. Since the purpose of the reading was all about Bebe, I tried to remain invisible and quiet in the corner. As the psychic starting tapping into Bebe's energy, however, she suddenly looked up, her eyes darting back and forth around her living room as if it had been invaded. Her mouth was open with amazement, and while Bebe and I could not see anything, I did feel a significant change in the energy.

The psychic then turned to us in puzzlement and asked if we could explain why her living room was suddenly full of Mayan spirits! Bebe merely rolled her eyes. "Geez, Lori!" she said. "It is always about you and your Mayans."

I smiled, and then listened as the psychic reported there were several Mayan priests present who wanted to talk to me.

As I wanted to respect Bebe's reading, I told the Mayans that they needed to pick a better time. Though the psychic tried to continue the session, she reported that as much as I wanted them to leave, they were not going anywhere. When the session for Bebe finally ended, the psychic turned to me. "The Mayans insist that I tell you that they will be sending you something. You will receive the feather of a hyacinth macaw. This will be a powerful symbol to you now and in the future. Take it, knowing it is from them."

I remembered the vision of the feathered headdress and wondered if there was a connection to that.

Back in Scottsdale, I called Deborah, desperate to talk with Tino after all I had been through. Before opening a channel to him, however, she and I talked about the whole experience I'd had in Colombia. She had been as much my lifeline as Bebe was while I was there. There were too many calls even to mention throughout the process of my spiritual transition and I was grateful for her standing by when I needed her.

Our session began with Deborah describing Tino as less testy and without the same urgency to run the show as in previous sessions. He was becoming surer of Deborah's integrity in transmitting his thoughts in the most appropriate way. I think the way she handled herself during my crisis was also a huge step for both Tino and me in realizing that Deborah's intentions were always for the highest good.

As usual, I got right to the point and told Tino that I needed to know his perspective on what had happened to me over the past several months. He said there was an amazing current of energy around me, and that it had swirled and swirled as I was traveling through the process. "You were living a nightmare, and I wanted to find the SOB who was behind this," Tino said. "I saw you so helpless and powerless. I tried to reach you, and although I thought you could hear me, the messages were too mixed up with all the other voices that were talking to you. I knew you were confused and didn't know who you were talking to.

"I wasn't aware of what was really happening to you—or even aware this could happen to people, especially to you and me. What a revelation to know these things can actually occur!"

Deborah then encouraged us not to dwell on these matters, since I was still vulnerable. Moving back into those energies could have a negative impact on me she pointed out, since the experience was still so fresh.

Tino agreed and instead told me the changes going on since we had last chatted. He said he was learning to listen—and when he did there was so much to learn! He had gone through a big revelation, jokingly sharing that he finally realized he really did not know everything! This brought a big laugh from Deborah and me.

I could tell that he had been busy watching life reviews as he was bringing up scenes of our time together. In the spirit world the soul undergoes a "screening" of events from life. By doing this, the perception of his life deepens as he comes to better understand the impact he had on others. Life is a learning process.

The life review a soul undergoes often brings to the surface regrets of things that were not accomplished while in the realm we live in. Although this may be disappointing, the regret is not typically accompanied by deep sadness, as the perception in the spirit world involves viewing things from a macro-sense that helps spirits to realize that anything they did was all part of their life plan, or fate.

During this conversation, I realized that Tino's sense of who I was had been expanding as he watched and learned in depth about the real me. He had realized my strengths and the compassion I had for him during his illness. He no longer had barriers around what he would share with me.

Without an audience vying for his attention on the other side, he was also gaining a better understanding of who he really was. He was no longer the performer and entertainer. This took some getting used to. Going to the other side was a solitary journey of deep reflection even though there were spirit teachers there to help him take responsibility for his growth. He also realized that his relationship with me had been his greatest lesson so far. "To know you from this perspective and see all you did for me—with so little gratitude from me—has been very humbling. I just never found the words that I needed to say."

I asked Tino to tell me what it was like there, looking at me on Earth. He said there was a fluorescent light around me. "In the dimension where I live, there are vibrant colors like flowers and autumn leaves. Everything is alive! This surprises me. Although there is light, it does not come from any kind of sun."

Tino reported that the "air" where he was, was slightly warm, with breezes, although there was no wind. "There are places to sit and people strolling through parks. Everything has a different composition than on Earth. I'm enjoying traveling around, but I haven't figured out how all that works. There are projects here, there is grass, and I am able to create a boat to ride around in. I do not need to eat, but if I want the pleasure of eating, it is available to me. The taste of a good scotch is a memory I enjoy.

"I have seen some friends I had while on Earth. I have a place that I create from my mind that is like a home, but I am not there all of the time. I get around. I enjoy seeing the pets that transitioned from my life to here, and there is a sense of merriment and a festive atmosphere as only the higher emotional vibrations, like gratitude and love, are here. I do not miss my body, and most beings here find it frustrating that loved ones focus so much on tending to their graves when they rarely are there.

"The weather is perfect for whatever I like to do, therefore it does not affect my activities. I play golf, but it was a challenge at first not to be in my body. What I do instead is create the scene of a golf game and I am a manipulator of energies that create a competitive scenario. I can then create others to play with and I orchestrate a game. It is kind of like playing a video game except I use my mind to create an outcome. After I win—as I always do—I especially enjoy creating a hole-in-one celebration at the nineteenth hole.

"You would be thrilled to know that I no longer need a siesta since my body and mind are no longer tired.

"Now, about getting into heaven. There are no criteria for admittance. Everyone is welcome. And there is no preferential hierarchy established for those who have conducted themselves well on Earth according to their own view of perfection. Imagine my relief," he said, then chuckled. "What I guess I missed the most when coming here was the human feeling of being alive, as well as the parties and friends. But I learned quickly that those desires were when my ego was in command and control. Coming here destroys the ego."

He could hear my next question without me asking it, and said, "Yes, of course, when you call me I am there and especially when you are sad I feel that energy and it draws me to you. I admit I think of you a lot," he added.

When I asked if death was harder for him or for me here on Earth, he answered quickly, "Oh, Lori, it is much harder for those left behind! There are so many emotions you must work through. The sense of loss is not the same here. Nothing here is as deep as the pain in a human heart. That is where we all experience suffering. Here, there are only vibrations moving between us, so the sense of aloneness is different for you than for me. Emotions are not the same. I can touch into your vibration and that allows me to understand better and have a richer communication with you than before but it is not the same for you.

"For me, my time on Earth was very brief although it may have seemed full at seventy-seven. In the greater scheme of things, it was a quick trip when you compare that time with an eternity. Earth is like signing up for a master's degree. The whole purpose of going there is to learn and the process begins when you show up.

"I learned from my experiences that before we come to Earth we have a prebirth planning session in which we outline the lessons we want to learn. It is kind of like choosing a template of karma we wish to experience. After we have planned our journey, picked our parents, and set in motion the trip, the soul enters the body of a child at varying times during the gestation period. Prior to this, the soul remains in the spirit realm.

"After we are born, from birth to age seven, we form opinions and beliefs and establish right from wrong, this defines our culture, religion, and customs. This is when we form our definitions of love. From age seven to fourteen, we learn the importance of relationships, and through those relationships we learn about power, control, jealousy, betrayal, guilt, and blame. In our teenage years, we develop the ego, which prospers in the survival mode as we develop arrogance and set boundaries. Here we can become flexible or inflexible, positive or negative in our approach.

"Finally, we end up in the heart where we have hopefully learned to trust, have compassion and forgiveness for others, and learn to love ourselves. This is the most elusive destination on the planet and where all of us need support to get there. Arriving at living from the heart is a complicated journey, which requires that we cut through the negative layers of learning that destroy the ego. The journey to the heart is like *baklava:* You get layers of sweetness, but also a lot of nuts thrown in. When we become immersed in the fears of our entire soul group, or family, this is like wearing an overweight backpack on your earthly journey. The human body suffers from deterioration and creates disease that results from hauling around fear-based emotions.

"It is unfortunate that we fall so easily into fear, yet we are instinctively 'hardwired' to escape injury or death. The tragedy of our existence is that the current human condition results in covering up our souls with layers of unnecessary fear. This separates us from the Earth. When the mind is free, there is no attachment to what others may layer atop the innocence of who we are, so we love and prosper beyond our imaginations.

"I realize that we are all in perfection when we arrive and when we leave. The easiest way to get through the Earth experience as unscathed as possible is to ignore irrelevant fears, accept change, forgive everyone, and show gratitude even when it seems impossible. By accepting the notion that coming to Earth was a commitment to work on the evolution of your fears, and hopefully the destruction of your ego, it will set you free. Some manage it better than others. Although there are some electives and free time, the only way to graduate is to die. All those on Earth are experiencing many different levels of this enlightenment, which makes for quite a scene!"

Tino had given me a sense of his perspective now, he saw things from a bigger picture and the details of the human life journey were not as significant to his thinking. It was all just a process and journey that every time we spoke, he was becoming more aware of.

What I had learned in Colombia was that the only way to know good was to know evil, and the only way to know true love was to face fear. These opposing forces were essential to the process of learning on Earth. It was very reassuring knowing that every step I took was a learning process. I needed to embrace it no matter how crazy it seemed. This was the way to come into the knowledge of ourselves and shed our conditioning. By suffering, we know better about taking a positive view of life's experiences, which enriches our education and opens us up to loving ourselves and others.

I knew the journey of the shamanic world would be to find the "real me," the honey beneath the layers of nuts in my baklava. It would be a life of pain and suffering if I did not allow the emergence of my gifts and my true self. I knew my next step would be to rise from the layers of depression and fear of being alone and find my oneness.

Upon reflection, this was how Tino lived on Earth. And apparently, he continued to live this way. He would have cringed at the use of the word *dead* to describe his current existence. It was not a term that he felt reflected his state of being now.

CHAPTER EIGHTEEN

I N DESCRIBING WHAT WAS happening to me, some people would say, "You have a *gift*." Originally I thought it
was strange to use the word gift to describe the spiritual
sensitivity and perceptions I now had, considering all the
troubles I went through because of them. In time, I came
to understand why. Most enlightened people call the ability
to communicate with dead people a gift, as it means that
the barriers between our world and the spiritual world have
disintegrated for them. This leads to a new way of seeing.
The jury was out as to whether or not I would see my new
perceptions as a gift, as I still found myself facing many challenges in my daily life because of my mental state.

One of the more debilitating experiences occurred
when I went to an outdoor mall to get a manicure and
pedicure. Now living with my senses of touch, sight, sound,
taste, and smell on high alert, this would be my first challenge to have someone touching me.

A young man was doing my pedicure. As he was rub-
bing a soft lotion on the dry skin of my legs and arms, the
energy from his hands began to penetrate me. I could see

a scene in Southeast Asia. The feeling grew stronger and stronger until I felt my body becoming overheated. My skin was almost burning! Because of this, I was feeling a sense of fear and growing more uncomfortable by the minute.

Anxiously, I asked the young man where he was from, and he said, "Cambodia." Digging deeper, I asked why he had left there, and he told me some of his family had been killed by landmines and his home was burned.

The energy of death and the fear of landmines continued to permeate my skin even deeper, until I could no longer take it. Despite my half-painted toenails, I paid the bill and stumbled out the door. I walked down the sidewalk in fear that I was going to step on a landmine. I could not make it to my car, so I went into a furniture store, where I sat on a couch until the energy of the man's touch dissipated and I was able to go home.

On another occasion, while I was having lunch with a friend, a girl walked across the restaurant and approached me, rather upset. She asked why I was taking pictures of her with my iPhone. I looked at the phone and saw a light on, which made me wonder if it was malfunctioning. I checked to see if there were any photos taken and there was nothing, I guess just the light was flashing at her.

An Apple store was nearby so I went and asked the tech guys to check my phone. They took it apart and removed the battery, yet the light remained on. In total amazement the clerk finally said, "Lady, there is nothing powering this phone, but the light is still on! I'll need to send this to Cupertino so they can see this!"

I grabbed my phone and the battery and left. They already had several of my laptops in Cupertino. I got to my car, staring at the blinking light on my phone, and tried again to wrap my mind around the idea that with just my presence I was able to power electronic devices! The same thing had been happening at home. Lights would go on and off, and my smoke alarm would beep for no reason—all because I passed by.

This happened with increasing frequency. I would try to purchase things with my credit cards and the cash register systems were not able to process the transaction. At times it would charge strange amounts or none at all. I would walk through parking lots and car alarms would go off. It was funny at times, but usually annoying. Phone calls were also strange, as I would hear weird sounds or voices interrupting, depending on who was at the other end of the line.

My life was a constant barrage of energy, and it became exhausting. I tried to ignore it, but couldn't. I wanted to be able to manage all the energies I was sensing, but I did not know how. Every day was a new adventure in discovering how I affected things and how things affected me.

There were beautiful moments with spirit as well, which I will always cherish. For example, on Valentine's Day, I was feeling very sad about being alone and was just leaving a parking lot when I felt Tino's swooping presence. "Go into Target." he said, and though I really was not in a great mood, I figured I might as well see what he was up to. I stood in the store and said, "Okay, what now?" Tino told me to go to the checkout counter, so I headed there without anything to purchase until I saw fresh bouquets of roses near the counter. It was Tino's way of saying, "Happy Valentine's Day!"

Tino then said, "Lori, please have roses in the house at all times—from me, for all the times I never sent them." It was a tender moment and I was very happy for the memory. When I got home there was an email from Deborah that Tino had shown up and suddenly there was the smell of roses all around her. Tino had then showed her a vision of peach roses, which of course were the same color as the ones he had told me to buy. These were the times that I welcomed my gifts, as I was able to enrich my life by interacting with those on the other side.

After all the scary things happened to me, I was very aware of my need for spiritual protection. I began reading more about helpful spirit guides and angels. The next day I decided to look for a spiritual bookstore that had been recommended to me. I liked the idea of talking to a real person about some good books to read. I found a sweet little store, A Peace of the Universe, where I met the owner, a gentle woman named Judith. The store was full of light, just as she was. Books on crystals, fairies, and angels lined the shelves. We had a nice chat about all those things, and she suggested some books. I could sense she was a loving person as she shared stories about spending her weekends at a dog shelter. I was so taken by these stories that I promised to stop by again to make a donation.

The following week, I stopped by the shop with things for the shelter. Judith was pleased that I had returned. She put her arm around me, saying there was something she had been keeping for years that she wanted to give me. I was intrigued. She returned from the back room and handed me a large Ziploc bag. "I think these are for you."

The bag contained two hyacinth macaw feathers. "I don't know why, Lori," she said, "but for some reason I think these feathers are very important to you." I immediately felt the presence of the Mayans near me. A powerful energy came through my body as I took the feathers from the bag and held them in my hands. Speechless and humbled, I placed the feathers over my heart in gratitude.

Judith smiled. "Look, Lori, they even match your outfit!" I looked down at my blue jeans with my blue blouse and the yellow leather pouch of stones around my neck for protection. I was yellow and blue, just like the hyacinth macaws!

I knew I needed support from the other side to function, so I signed up for a class in Scottsdale with an expert on angels. The class was designed to teach how to connect with angels and develop a relationship with them for a sound spiritual life.

One of our first exercises was to sit facing a partner and call in Raphael, the archangel that governs healing. The teacher emphasized the importance of not getting in the way of the message, and to share whatever came through, no matter how strange it might seem.

My partner, whose name I don't remember, was a lovely woman from Canada. I went first, summoned Raphael, and immediately saw a very deep emerald-green color envelop me. I was then given a picture in my mind's eye of the woman across from me in a belly dancing outfit. I took a look at the woman and thought this image was rather far out, but held to the instructions and expressed what I had seen.

As I shared the image, the woman's mouth opened in wonder and her eyes began twinkling with joy. I had clearly touched on something. She asked me what color the belly dancing outfit was. When I told her it was green and had glittery coins around it, she broke out laughing. "Oh, my god! Last week I ordered a belly dancing outfit and signed up for a class that starts after I get home from this seminar!" I had a good laugh then, too, and learned a big lesson about trusting messages from spirits.

When my partner asked for the meaning of the message, my spirits told me that it was time for her to enjoy life and expand herself beyond the limitations of the mind. She was obviously well on her way.

Always wanting to learn more, I searched the internet for someone I could talk to about shamanism, which led me to visit Canyon Ranch, a health spa in Tucson. There I met the resident shaman and asked her to help me understand what a shaman really is. She explained that a shaman is a person who is able to move into altered states of consciousness to access the spirit world for the purpose of obtaining healing powers and information. I felt that this was much of what I had been experiencing.

The shaman I met told me that the word *shaman* comes from Siberia and means "someone who sees in the dark." In the past, spiritual healers and seers were a tribe's only medicine people. A shamanic practice in the present-day world, I learned, is built on the foundation that all problems—physical, emotional, or mental—are caused by spiritual imbalances. Shamans use many methods, such as soul retrieval, extraction of unwanted energy, divination, psychopomp (helping people who have died to go into the light that leads to the other side), hands-on healing, and the use of herbs and potions. Their goal is to help their clients restore their energetic balance. Shamans always work with spiritual allies who guide the process of healing. Shamans are conduits for the work of benevolent spiritual guides, whose healing energy comes through them.

Last, but not least, she told me that a shaman can journey to where souls are.

Now that got my attention!

We had several meetings during the week and I was hopeful that this woman could provide answers for my most burning question: "Why me?" I was continuing to have visions of being among thousands of Mayans in ceremonies, and starting to feel I had a responsibility to them in some way, but that answer was still elusive.

I felt as if the light beam that had struck my body months earlier was a catalyst designed to expose something very deep inside me. I could also sense the energy of beings that were threatened by the power of the Mayans that came through me. I was realizing more and more that there were consequences to the new vibration of energy that I was carrying.

When I asked for more answers, the Canyon Ranch shaman suggested that I make a shamanic journey to find the truth, and I agreed. To do the journey, I would lie on a bed while consciousness-shifting music played. The process sounded easy, as I had been in many altered states by then. She promised to stay with me and guide me throughout my journey.

I was quickly in a trance state where it was first shown to me that Tino and I had shared many lifetimes together. We were kindred souls. Our favorite lifetime was when we were brothers, and we have been together in every lifetime ever since this one in some way.

In this lifetime however, the karmic connection between us was based on the time we were Mayans. As we began the session, I was taken to a scene in the jungles of Central America. The place was in shambles, with Spanish soldiers strolling casually among dead bodies and looting treasures. I was a leader of the people in the scene we found ourselves in.

In another scene, in an adobe house, the leather hide that served as a door was pulled back, revealing a man lying on the floor in depreciating health. That figure was me in that distant lifetime. Having contracted small pox from the invading forces, I was dying. As I lay there suffering, there was a man kneeling next to me, attending to my needs and trying to heal me. That man was my beloved Tino, who was a kind and loving brother to me.

This lifetime was the key to the visions that I had been seeing. The circumstances explained the many negative emotions I had felt during my awakening process toward the Spaniards and the Catholic Church.

I continued my intention to receive more information and the vision continued. Tino was born into this lifetime with the soul memory of terrible grief because he had been unable to save me in our shared Mayan lifetime. His intention at birth was to teach me to love beyond love—to hold him and then be able to let him go. His task also was to draw me back to Lake Ilopango. We were karmically connected. I would compensate him for his previous service to me by taking care of him and keeping him alive as long as I did.

Still curious about the man lying on the bed in the adobe hut dying of smallpox, I intentionally looked around and there it was again, a beautiful headdress made of hyacinth macaw feathers, on the dirt floor beside me. The surroundings were not elegant. Even though I seemed to be a man of great importance, I had been confined to a simple hut. This explained my lifetime fear of losing everything.

The scene was emotionally shattering, so I started crying. Immediately the shaman asked me to switch to a different scene. This time the Mayan ancestors came through and showed me how the energy of the world would shift its vibration after 2012—the year when the Mayan calendar would end—at which point we would begin to see a transformation of humanity as it exists. Since we would experience this as a crisis, it was important that as many human beings as possible reach higher stages of enlightenment to endure the cosmic storm of change that was coming. They made it clear that although they had cracked me open, the change in me would serve a greater purpose than myself. They were explaining that now that I was "lit up" it would be necessary to sustain a higher level of my human vibration to complete the work that they had planned for me. The unfortunate outcome of this would be that I was still extremely vulnerable to energies of lower frequency.

CHAPTER NINETEEN

A FTER MY SESSION WITH the shaman at the spa, I returned to the house where I was staying. It was a horrible night. I lay on my back in bed, staring into the darkness as negative spirits surrounded me. I grew frightened because I could hear their threatening voices. The energy around me was fluctuating and I was in trouble. I felt trapped and lured in, and I had a sense that worse was yet to come.

All night the voices I heard were angry and evil. I sensed retaliation was going on, but for what? The only thing I could think of was that there were forces that did not want me to accomplish a task other spirits had planned for me. I knew that the forces opposing me were strong, so I tried using my skills of protection. But everything I did only seemed to make things worse. It was as if more and more negative energies were being recruited for the attack.

Morning finally arrived and I walked to the room where I had been meditating and working on my connections to the angels. I felt like something was being planned to provoke me and I was afraid. First, I started to lose the feeling in both of my legs. As numbness crept up each leg,

I managed to walk to the back yard with a comforter I pulled off the bed, and sat on the warm gravel. In hopes of warming my legs and getting the feeling in them back, I began piling rocks over them, but the numbness had already reached my thighs. I then covered my body with the comforter and made a little tent to sit in.

I guess I was creating a sweat lodge, but at the time I did not know what a sweat lodge was. I had a bowl of sage that I lit on fire, and the smoke began to fill the inside of the comforter. I was coughing and sweating, but didn't care, because I felt protected in that small space.

I stayed there and burned all of the sage I had, and the numbness started to subside until I was finally able to walk again. I got up to go back to the house, but suddenly something or someone pushed me into the pool. I looked around frantically and saw no one. Then I felt a hand pushing my head under the water. Splashing my way to the shallow end of the pool, I put my feet on the bottom and was trying to reach some balance when a tablet of chlorine was shoved into my mouth. The voices told me never to speak to anyone about the things the Mayans had told me.

I managed to get the chlorine tablet out of my mouth and then tried desperately to wash out my mouth before the undiluted chlorine reached my stomach and possibly killed me. Because I was suddenly in for a fight for my life with an unseen enemy, I called in every form of protection I knew. Angels, saints, Jesus, Mary—you name them, I called them in. Only then was I finally able to get myself out of the pool.

Things were still spinning, but I felt I had made some progress. I needed to eat something because of the chlorine, and I was still very dizzy, so I cracked a few eggs and cut up some tomatoes to make scrambled eggs. But I wasn't safe yet. Shortly after I turned on the stove, while the burner was hot, something grabbed my head and smashed it right into the hot burner!

Desperately I tried to lift up my head and finally did, only to discover that my forehead was burned and bleeding. I also realized my hair was on fire. I grabbed some scissors, and started to cut off the damaged hair.

When I looked around and saw no one else there with me, my mind had no resources to understand what was happening. For this reason, I knew I had crossed the threshold of insanity. The resolve that kept me alive throughout the ordeal kicked in and I determined that I was going to find whoever was responsible, seen or unseen. I held a knife in my hand, ready to protect myself.

I went to the front porch to see if anyone had entered from there, and at that moment a neighbor walked by and saw me with the knife, a burned forehead, blood all over my face, and much of my hair cut off. She became frantic and worried, and asked what was going on with me. But since I only stared back at her in silence, she rushed to call 911.

The emergency responders came, and of course, the scene looked like I had tried to kill myself. I could hear the voices laughing at me, as they had accomplished what they set out to do. No matter what I said to anyone at that point, I appeared crazy, so it was futile to talk. There was no reasonable explanation for what had just happened.

The paramedics put me in the back of the ambulance and tried to take a sample of my blood. As I saw the foil pouch being opened and the "stick" being readied to test my blood, it was the moment of reaching tilt from my trauma levels and I broke into a million mental pieces. A hurricane of post-traumatic images came funneling through me, especially visions of all the days I spent with Tino and the diabetic testing, shots, cures, and everything else I had done to save him. I grabbed all the medical supplies that were stored in the ambulance and threw them on the floor, telling the paramedics to stay away from me. They continued to insist on the tests, but I refused to let them touch me.

I have little recollection of getting to the hospital, but when I arrived at the emergency room the sound of the equipment and the beeping machines took me right back to the New York emergency room where I had spent several days begging the staff for a room for Tino.

The hospital staff insisted on doing a rape test. My legs were spread after I was strapped down and restrained on an examination table. I continued to fall deeper into the trauma and I looked between my two restrained knees into the hall-way—and there was Farides, in spiritual form. She seemed to be working behind scenes, trying to save me.

After the test, I fell into a deep trance, as my soul could not survive how I was feeling and where I was anymore. I began to watch a movie of my life as if on a spliced reel of film going forward and backward, stopping on different scenes. It started in childhood, then went to high school, then to the time in El Salvador when I was stalked, back to grade school, over to a bomb blast that went off near my car, a bad time in college, having AK47s pointed at my head by guerrillas, almost drowning in the ocean when I was thrown out of a fishing boat, crashing in a hot air balloon, dead bodies around my house during the Salvadoran civil war, and back to my childhood when a man followed me home from grade school, and on and on with troubling images, until I ended up back in my mother's womb in the hospital in Hawaii where I was born.

The womb was a calm place, with water sloshing around me and nutrients from the umbilical cord filling me up with bliss and satisfaction. I could hear the sounds of the hospital around me, but I was fine because I was safe and ready to be born.

Overnight, the doctors pumped me full of antipsychotic drugs. Upon waking early the next morning, I found myself on a gurney in a makeshift room for "mental cases." There were other marginal and presumably undiagnosed patients around me who needed the watchful eye of a young nurse who instead had her eyes on a book she was reading.

I sensed I was in a hospital when I saw the nurse, and I remember asking her where Tino was. She said she did not know, but I believed they had hidden him somewhere in the hospital and I needed to find him. My determination to search for Tino resulted in me being drugged again, and remaining incoherent until I was ready to be released and moved. I asked over and over where I was being taken, but no one gave me an answer I could comprehend. I was desperate to stay where I was and wait for Tino, but soon I was in an ambulance on my way to a mental facility—just as Oscar and Farides had warned I might be.

The ambulance backed up to the entrance of the Tucson mental health facility where I was pushed out on a gurney. Someone helped me down and told me to sit in a wheelchair. *Am I sick? Injured? What am I doing in a wheelchair?* I kept asking myself. I was then taken into a small examining room and told to wait. It looked like a doctor's office with boxes of Band-Aids and gauze, and things for testing.

A nurse came in and told me I would be tested for intake. Since I was now thoroughly drugged, the flood of memories of past hospital stays was finally subsiding. I was relatively calmer than when I had arrived at the emergency room the day before. They tried to take a blood test, but when I looked down at my fingers they morphed into Tino's hand. I was confused as to who was being tested.

I wasn't quite sure where I was or why I was there. I did not feel sick so it seemed strange to be in a hospital gown. A nurse handed me a plastic bag holding my clothes and told me to get dressed. Then I was escorted to another room where I waited for a psychiatric evaluation.

A man came in with a clipboard. I was not sure who he was since titles and labels of people no longer made any sense to me. If someone told me she or he was a doctor it meant nothing. The only way I could distinguish others was by their bodies and the energy field around them. This doctor started by asking if I heard voices, and I said yes. At that answer, his eyebrows raised. A slight shake of the head told me I had provided the wrong answer. I sensed my response made him unsure, and a few more questions and answers seemed to elicit the same energetic response.

My thoughts seemed much better at getting my point across so I tried sending answers to the doctor telepathically. When he did not respond, I was frustrated. He kept asking me to talk to him and answer his questions, and I kept sending him the answers telepathically, but he would not write down my responses.

Moreover, the voices then told me not to speak at this time, as people were not going to understand me. So I deliberately became quiet. When I stopped communicating I was deemed to be catatonic, a diagnosis that would change my status and move me to a higher-level security designation, whereupon the state could severely limit my rights about my care and my ability to be released.

I continued to remain silent, but I soon became concerned that I was going to go too deep into a system I would not easily escape. The voices, however, told me to continue to be quiet because help was on the way.

I then felt the presence of angelic beings. I specifically do not use the word *angels,* as these beings did not look and feel like the stereotypical forms I had seen in pictures. They were more like spirits, but with energies that penetrated my heart chakra. Their presence was around me and I was lifted into a state of no worries, no anxiety—nothing but the feeling of love, as you might sense it while looking into the eyes of a puppy.

The doctor continued his attempt to get me to talk, but I was focused on the energies around me.

The door flung open and another, very energetic man walked in, asking how things were going. The first man said, "She's in a catatonic state. She just keeps staring at me and the only question she said yes to was that she hears voices."

Mr. Energy took my chart and glanced at it, seeing that I was from El Salvador. He said that he was from Venezuela, and then asked me in Spanish if I spoke Spanish. I was quiet and started listening to the voices, which told me to say, *"Si,"* which I did. So he started speaking Spanish to me. I felt this was the person the angelic beings had sent to help me and a sense of trust came over me.

The voices told me to answer his questions in Spanish, so when he asked again, "Do you hear voices?" I made a face like I was thinking. What I was really doing was listening to the voices who were advising me what the best answer would be. I repeated what they told me. "Yes, I hear voices."

Mr. Energy then asked me how often and under what circumstances. I listened to the voices and repeated what they said: "When I listen to my iPod."

Both of the men laughed. They asked me again if it was ONLY when I had my earphones on and I told them exactly as I was told, *"Si."*

Mr. Energy grabbed my chart and drew a line through the words "possible schizophrenia," saying with a sense of deep compassion, "She's going to be fine. We should have spoken to her in Spanish since she's been living in Latin America for twenty-five years. Leave her in this facility and I'll work with her."

Another man walked me to the end of a long hallway to my room. I unenthusiastically picked up my few belongings, which were now contained in a plastic bag, and followed him. A large woman was asleep and snoring in the twin bed next to what would be my bed.

I had been up over twenty-four hours. I was exhausted and needed rest. As I lay down to sleep, soft, gentle voices came to me, saying, "You will need to rid yourself of all your fears of death to get out of here." The voices said they would move me to another place and the process would take care of the last ounces of fear I had.

I was in total surrender at that point and said, "That's fine. I'm ready to go."

As I lay quietly on the bed in the room I'd been given, all of a sudden the feeling in my toes was gone. The absence of all energy and sensation continued moving up my legs, through my pelvis, until I could not move the bottom half of my body. I was again paralyzed. The loss of energy then moved toward my chest, but seemed to go around my heart, as it made its way up to my neck, then stopped. I seemed to stop breathing, yet it wasn't uncomfortable. None of this caused me any anxiety. The feeling of being paralyzed continued. Soon I was gone to the world, unconscious for the entire night.

The next morning, I woke up thinking I was in heaven, even though it looked very much like my new room at the mental facility. I was capable of seeing and feeling the interconnectivity of energy between everything. The only window was the one on the door at the end of the long hallway outside of my room, so I ventured to take a look outside of it. It was already daylight. There was a bunch of sand and a fence.

Heaven looked a lot like Tucson.

The distinctions between day and night were no longer relevant to me. Time was completely lost. This brought me no sense of urgency. The energy for getting somewhere was gone, so there was nothing pushing me to do anything. My body and mind had no sense of being "on time."

Since I was no longer in a hurry, I walked slowly toward a wall displaying artwork done by previous patients. I spent hours looking at the drawings, as each line, picture, color, and image meant something to me. I could also sense the emotion that accompanied each drawing. Each piece of artwork had an intricate and detailed message for me. The colors were also very significant; each one carried its own energy. Everything in the pictures was relevant: lines, shapes, sizes, textures, type of paper, the energy behind the stroke of the pen, crayon, or pencil, the smell of the medium. From the tiniest dot to the whole of the drawing, it all had a connection to me.

I remember thinking how amazing it was that all the previous patients knew I was planning on being there and had been thoughtful enough to leave these very personalized drawings for me to see.

I continued to walk the halls, at times encountering fellow patients. Some had chemical imbalances in their brains that I could sense, while others had cellular dysfunction due to ingesting foreign substances. I was able to sense all the things that did not belong in their bodies. But if I focused on their energy fields for too long, whatever was ailing them would start to manifest in me, so I shut off my focus and kept moving along.

I saw a group of people congregating by a doorway and felt anticipatory energy surrounding them. That seemed strange to me since I myself had no sense of urgency. The doors opened and everyone went rushing past me. I followed them through. I was the last one to arrive in the cafeteria. I could smell food, which was intoxicating. All the aromas came flowing into my nostrils and I felt hungry, but still I felt no urgency.

It was my turn at the buffet station so I picked up my tray and saw all the different offerings, each with its own separate energy. The more colorful and brighter the food, the more energy it displayed, so fruits and vegetables and the bright bags of chips especially drew my attention. Other foods, like potatoes and other starches and meat, felt heavy and dense. It seemed that if I picked them up they would weigh so much that I might not be able to carry them. Processed foods gave me the feeling of uncertainty so I skipped them as well.

The different beverages all had another energetic footprint that made me wary, so I settled for water from the dispenser. But I had doubts about the water because I could see that the tubes inside the machine had residue, and I knew that the water passing through it did not arrive in a perfect state. I sipped it carefully to avoid any negative effects.

For my first meal, I chose all the colorful stuff as it seemed to have the "best energy." Then I sat down alone to eat. Other patients sat at tables alone, as if caught up in their own silence just as I was. I really was not up for talking, but if someone had wanted to chat with me telepathically that would have been fine.

I walked back to my room after breakfast. My roommate was still asleep. I could sense the medications in many of the patients there, which kept them in nonresponsive states and therefore in their rooms asleep. She was one of those people.

I looked down at my finger to a woven gold band Tino had bought me on a trip to Italy. I remember thinking it was nice and shiny, but it truly held no material value for me anymore. Looking at gold brought me no sense of importance. I could feel that my roommate had economic problems. In fact, I knew everyone's issues if I chose to focus on them, so it seemed very illogical that I had this ring when this woman needed it much more than I did. I took the ring off and very carefully put it on her finger while she slept. It was a tad snug, but that gave me security that it would not fall off. She got a little restless and threw her arms off the bed, but the ring stayed on. I had lost touch with the value of all material things. I was no longer a part of the system of acquisitions and valuing importance by what I had. That was all lost to me. Everything that motivated me in life until then had disappeared. I was no longer held captive by my material wants or previous monetary desires.

I passed time in the hospital attending classes and creativity sessions. I have no recall as to what purpose they had, or if they were even relevant to my state of being. I was not aware of the diagnosis the staff had labeled me with. When the instructors spoke I would often get caught up in their personal energy and conflicts. I had better knowledge of others through feelings than through words.

I could see that many of the drug-related patients had entities attached to their bodies. One time I asked an entity why he was there. He explained that many of the roads in Tucson do not have sidewalks or bike paths, and because of the pleasant climate and beautiful scenery, many people ride bikes. He said that there were a couple of entities hanging out at the mental hospital because they had been hit by cars and killed instantly. For some reason they would seek the weak in this mental hospital to find new hosts they could attach themselves to. This explained why I could sense dual identities in some of the patients.

Many of the entities I saw were spirits that had not properly crossed over to the other side at death. Later, I would come to understand that spirits in the "middle world" (our world) often look for those who are addicts or emotionally unstable so that they can draw energy from them and have the sensation of being connected to a body. These were not the same spiritual entities that had attacked me back at my house. They were more like lost souls.

Daily life in the mental facility was a matter of balancing energies for me. Since I could feel negative and positive in everything and everyone around me, I walked a fine line to keep my own energy in check. Needless to say, I was so overloaded by emotions and sensations that I was exhausted at the end of every day.

My key to leaving the institution ultimately would depend on my ability to rebalance my energy and build it to overflowing in my favor.

One area of contention I had with the institution was its dispensing of medications. When I checked in I was given a wristband containing a barcode. The nurses were required to scan it any time they administered medicine in order to validate the list of the medications I was taking through their computer. But I would present my wrist and more than half the time the scanner light would turn red, not green, as was necessary to receive my meds. Sometimes the barcode scanner was green, then red, and then green! This happened over and over again, to the point that I grew concerned that they were giving me the wrong medications or wrong doses.

The helpful voices were telling me not to take medication, as it would be harder for me to listen to them and accomplish my purpose for being there.

I recalled the movie *One Flew over the Cuckoo's Nest* and the encounter between Nurse Ratched, played by Louise Fletcher, and Randle McMurphy, played by Jack Nicholson. I remembered how McMurphy would put the meds under his tongue, swallow a glass of water, and make his way to the nearest garbage can to throw the meds away. This I also did with much success for the majority of the time, so I was able to stay in a trancelike state and connected to the energetic forces around me.

I trusted the voices and spirits that were working with me more than any medicine. I also learned that as long as I kept quiet and did not express myself, I could function quite well.

CHAPTER TWENTY

THE SPIRITS WOULD WAKE me up in the morning, insist-ing that I walk up and down the halls during most of my free time. When I asked them why they wanted me to do this, they told me that I was healing people and helping them leave the institution. Every day I felt more and more powerful, and since I myself was still running on an over-dose of energy from the beam of light that hit me it seemed logical that I might have an effect on others. My rational mind was not sure if it really mattered, as the feeling of cause and effect was rather subtle to others, nonetheless I believed in my power to heal.

Every morning I had a dilemma about what to wear, but not because I was concerned about how I looked. It was actually a relief to have no mirrors around, as I was a mess. I could have been cast in the role of a mental character in a Hollywood movie with my burned forehead, sizzled eye-brows and eyelashes, and the most bizarre haircut I have ever had! My dilemma had to do with the energy of my clothing.

One morning I put on a red shirt and walked towards the nurse's station to ask some questions. The energy from the color red was so overwhelming, however, that I could sense their adverse reaction to it. The energy they emitted in response to me had no compassion or concern for my questions or me. In fact, the nurses backed off and ignored me. I knew it was the color of the shirt, so I went back to my room and changed into a light pink blouse. Then I went back to the station again and got a totally different reaction.

I was beginning to verify that what was happening to me was having a direct effect on others.

After a few more days, I felt the pull of energy keeping me there, as if I was getting lost in the crowd. Now the computers were having difficulty finding my name at medicine time. The nurses said I was not in their system. When I showed up at meetings and they were taking roll call, my name would be the only one not on their list. For this reason, I was beginning to worry that maybe I would never get out of that place.

I kept falling through the cracks over and over again. Every day people were getting out, yet I was still there. When I asked how I could leave I was told that release came only with a doctor's orders. The doctor who had my case, however, would come and see patients, then leave without seeing me. When I would ask when he was supposed to see me, I was told that I was not on the list.

One day I waited by the door of the doctor's office and told him that I had not seen a doctor for days. He went to the nurse's station to verify what I said and they reluctantly confirmed it was true. Another day passed and the doctor promised to see me and again I was not on the list. While he was on his way out, I stopped and begged him to see me, but he was in a hurry so my case was again put off.

The next day I stood at the door of his office when he arrived and told him I insisted that he see me. He checked his computer list of patients and again I was not on his list! Commotion ensued because the computers near the nurse's station could not locate my name or my data, and nobody had any explanations as to why I did not appear anywhere.

Finally, the doctor agreed to see me and I went into his office. We had a nice talk. He confessed I had been totally misjudged by the system. "You came in here like a Scottsdale housewife who recently lost her husband, and the doctors categorized you as a possible overdose of antidepressants and a nervous breakdown."

At that moment, considering all I had been through, I would have given anything for that to be the real extent of my problem. The doctor then asked how long I had lived in El Salvador and if I had experienced any major traumas throughout my life. I rattled off the long list of traumatic episodes that I had experienced living in El Salvador. He sat back in astonishment when he heard what I recounted, and then asked if anyone in the hospital had ever asked me about these events before.

After I answered in the negative, he said, "Lori, looking at you no one would ever guess you have lived the kind of life you have. You look like such a 'normal' American that we totally ignored severe post-traumatic stress as a possibility."

My mind was thrilled to hear the word *normal* associated with me, even though the rest of me was still floating around the fourth and fifth dimensions of the universe. "I am going to diagnose you with post-traumatic stress disorder," the doctor said. "Hopefully, in a few days we can get you out of here so you can receive some private professional help. How does that sound?"

I was thrilled because I knew staying in that hospital would not resolve whatever was wrong with me.

Soon after my meeting with the doctor, one of the assistants came to my room and told me I was relocating to another room in the same annex. I sensed that the energy had shifted and that the winds were blowing in my direction. When I asked why I was being moved, he told me that my roommate had complained that I was showering too early in the morning— which was true, since my guides had me up and about walking through the halls healing everybody.

The assistant helped gather my things and walked me to my new room. A sweet young woman who had been admitted for severe alcoholism was there drying out. Her energy felt good, and I felt good going there, except there were a lot of spirits flying around in the room.

I did not have any of my shamanic tools with me—no sage, nothing—so I felt very vulnerable. I chatted with my new roommate, and as it was getting close to turning out the lights, I continued to watch spirits come in and out of the room. I approached the subject very cautiously and lightly asked, "Do you believe in spirits?"

We got going on the conversation until I was able to break the news that I could see things like that, and that I wanted to do a clearing of the room. She got a big smile on her face and asked, "Are you some kind of shaman or something?"

I laughed and simply answered, "Yes. Something like that."

The young woman told me I seemed afraid of not getting out of that place and I replied, "Yes, the energies seem to be keeping me here. Every time I want to leave I get pushed back." I then moved on to my urgency to clear the space.

"Go ahead and clear the energy in the room," she said. "I understand these things because my mom has studied shamanism and uses those methods in her practice. She is a psychiatric nurse and works in the Tucson medical system."

At that moment a massive grin appeared on my face! I knew I was in a safe place, and knew very well why I had been moved to this young woman's room. The energies since the psychic attack had finally fallen in my direction. So I cleared the room, talked to the spirits, and started moving the energy out.

I had no knowledge of what I did; it simply came to me out of pure intuition. But afterward, I finally slept through the night in a sweet calm.

The next morning, I was very content. The energy had truly changed and the voices speaking to me were gentle. I felt safe. I continued to walk up and down the halls for clearing. As was the case for most of the mornings since my arrival, I passed a young black man seated on the floor in the hallway with his arms wrapped around his knees and his head wedged between his arms, looking down at the linoleum. I sensed he had knowledge of things I also knew. My empathy for him was greater than for many of the others I encountered.

Every day we would all be taken outside for fresh air, and normally one of the assistants would get the young man and take him to a solitary place in the garden. I listened as the guides told me to sit next to him, which I did. Although he was a little uneasy with my energy at first, he soon lifted his head.

I could read his thoughts and it seemed like he could read mine.

I whispered to him, "You see cosmic butterflies like I do." The death in his eyes came to life, so I continued, "And because you see these butterflies, they think you're crazy." Then a sparkle appeared so I kept on, "I see them too, and they think I'm also crazy." Over the entire time of my transformation, butterflies had been showing up everywhere I went and their process of changing from caterpillar to butterfly was symbolic of what was happening to me. In Central America, the butterfly is a well-known motif in ancient Mayan relics.

In a quiet mumble, he asked, "How do know about them?"

I answered, "The spirit voices tell me all about these things, and I know, it's hard to turn off."

He finally turned his head to me and in complete coherency asked, "So what do you do?"

I replied, "I help other people understand it. I'm going to get you out of here."

"Really?" he said as I grabbed his arm, pulling him off the grass and moving him to a more secluded place to talk.

The young man told me how the voices had come to him describing that there would be a transformation of humanity. People were being spiritually awakened to this through the symbol of butterflies. He said his mother was a fanatic about raising butterflies and he had a total affinity with them. He also shared how, like me, he had lost his ability to discern what was real.

I advised him that he needed to start talking to the doctors and tell them he no longer heard the voices. "Tell them it's time for you to go home."

He nodded. Then we parted ways.

The next day the young man found me before his session with his doctor and I coached him into a comfort zone before he went to the meeting. I hoped for the best. When I saw him later he gave me a quick thumbs-up signal, so I knew it had gone well!

I was not able to have a lot of conversations with others. Since I was on the verge of getting out myself, I did not approach him for an explanation so as not to do anything to impede my departure.

Before the afternoon recess, my guides told me to bring a large glass of water outside with me so I could dunk my hand in it to inject it with healing energy. I was to place my intention on the sunlight, pull the energy through the crown of my head into my arms, and then put my hands into the water. In following the instructions, I felt angelic energy go through me.

I had seated myself next to the young man in the garden and this time he was very open to me and happy I was there.

The guides told me to sprinkle the water all over him, but because the assistants were always watching us I had to come up with a way to accomplish my task discreetly. I would dunk my hands in the water and then casually put my hands on his shoulder, his other shoulder, and his knees until I felt he had been truly nourished by it. Meanwhile, we casually chatted about transformation and butterflies, again comparing what the voices had been telling us.

I finally asked where the man was from and he responded, "I am a Blackfoot Indian from Montana." At that moment elation came over me, as I knew his heritage and my newfound Mayan heritage were somehow connected in the cosmology of things! I was fulfilling a purpose in healing him.

I told him, "Do everything I say and you will get out of here. Go home to your tribe and to your shamans. They will heal you, but get out of here, because you won't get better in this place. You belong with your tribe."

My young friend looked at me in shock, but he definitely got the message.

The next day I knew my Blackfoot friend had his release appointment. I was sending positive energy his way so he could get out. I looked around to see if he was in the cafeteria, but he was not there. As I was heading for the table with my tray, however, he came running across the room. As I put down my tray he grabbed me by the waist, almost lifting me in the air. "Thank you! Thank you! I am going home!" he said. His face was glowing and I was so happy for him. Later that afternoon, I saw him walk out the main door, smiling back at me as he left.

Every day people were leaving. The ward was getting quieter and quieter. I now knew that when my guides had me walking every day up and down the halls, it was making a difference. I was able to clear many of the entities I saw attached to the residents. People were getting better!

That was nice for those who were leaving, of course, but I still felt stuck, and there was always some delay or system glitch that kept me from leaving too.

I went into the library to have a heart-to-heart talk with my guides, who said, "Don't worry. You will get out." I thought it was a very strange way to put it, as if they knew my future without a doubt. I said, "So you mean you can see what happens to me after all of this?" and they answered, "Yes. Just stop the fear and you will get out. Go in the knowing that you get out, and you will get out."

It was all so complicated. Dump the fear and get out. Know beyond a shadow of a doubt that I get out, and I get out. See myself in the future out of there, and I get out. The guides were right that my power would diminish when fear crept in yet I could not help feeling vulnerable again and putting my head in my hands, I started to cry. After a few moments I looked up and saw my first roommate walk into the library, asking if she could talk to me. It was actually the first conversation that we had now that she was remarkably better and I was curious if she had noticed the ring. She sat at the table in front of me and asked, "Who are you?"

I answered, "I'm Lori, your old roommate. Remember?"

She said, "No, I am not talking about that. What I'm talking about is . . . what have you done to me?"

I thought, *Oh boy, now I'm in big trouble as she is going to cause problems with my exit strategy!* I tried to steer myself away from fear and assumptions and asked her to explain. She told me how she had lost her house, her family, everything, and was now living on the streets. She was losing her mind because she could not afford any medication; that was why she ended up in the mental ward.

She took off the ring I'd given her and placed it on the table, saying, "Someone put this ring on my finger and I started to get better."

I said, "That's great!"

She looked at me with curiosity as if I was keeping a secret from her, and then pressed on. "Do you know who gave me this ring? Did you see anyone come in our room and put it on my finger?

"Nope. No idea."

"I thought you had something to do with this."

I continued my lie, but soon she got very serious. "You have had an effect on people, especially me. I think that is why I am better and now get to leave this place."

The new me didn't praise myself for her comment, since my ego had been tossed in a dumpster in Colombia. I just smiled and wished her well. I told her she should pawn the ring and use the money to start a new life. She rose from the table and before walking out, looked back at me. "So I guess you are not going to tell me."

I replied, "Tell you what?"

She had a huge grin on her face and she walked away to pack and leave.

By this time, it was getting rather lonely around the ward. A lot more patients were leaving than were coming in, and I was still there.

This time I was alone in my room that night, since my roommate had been released earlier that day. I walked to the other side of the room and crossed through the moonlight coming from the hallway through my door, which was required to be left open. My thoughts went back to the multitude of nights I sat looking at the moon over Lake Ilopango, and I wondered if I would ever get back there. I had been stuck in the hospital system for almost two weeks by then. My family knew where I was, as they had been called about my case, but I had not spoken to them.

Reality was sinking in. I realized I did not know where my "stuff" was: my car, my suitcase, and the keys to my house—nothing. Even if I got out, I had no idea how I was going to get home. It was going to be a major reality check. I knew leaving would require me to explain to others outside the hospital what had happened.

I tried to reason my way around the experience that had brought me there. *Who had attacked me? Was it real or imagined? And whoever attacked me, why? Did I carry something inside me that had caused this reaction by energetic forces? Had the hours and hours of Mayan prophecies I'd been hearing given me knowledge that was spiritually sensitive? Who was talking to me? What did they want? Why me?*

The thoughts were whirling around like a vortex in my mind until I swirled into the energy itself and fell asleep, comforted by the memory of the message "Remember, you get out."

In the morning, I headed for breakfast. I was hopeful that this was the day of my release. I was given the opportunity to use the phone and the only phone number I could remember was Bebe's. In fear, I told her that if I did not get out within the next twenty-four hours, she should get on a plane and come get me. She said Oscar had called and wanted to know if she knew I was in a mental institution. She was shocked that he knew before she had a chance to tell him, since she and my parents and a very few other family members were the only people who knew what had happened to me. Her comments made me feel like the whole experience was premeditated.

I would soon realize that the call to Bebe was a big mistake. As soon as I got off the phone, I saw that I had put a load of doubt into the universe and that the dense energy of my words and hers would create a heavy force, like gravity, that could sabotage my exit.

Indeed.

My doctor showed up late and I pushed to see him first. "Where are you going from here?" he asked. That had a lovely ring to it, as it implied I was leaving. He then said, "You should go back to El Salvador and look for a mental health professional who can understand the traumatic events that put you here, especially since you were in a war during part of the time you lived there. Doctors here in the United States do not know the intricacies of living in violent countries. Lori, you have special needs."

I nodded in agreement with everything he said, keeping my eyes on his forefinger and thumb, which were wrapped around the pen that would give me my freedom. The pen moved every which way as he gave me suggestions about the next steps to take. Finally, after another agony of moments, I watched the pen hit the page with the word *RELEASE* glowing and pulsating at me! The doctor then moved the pen to the right side of the paper and scratched his signature on the line that sealed everything. At last I could go home!

I thanked the doctor for his help, and then followed him and his clipboard with my release paper toward the nurse's station . . . where he forgot to leave it on his way out! I politely raised my voice as he was just about out of the door, calling, "Doctor, please don't forget my paper!" He smiled and came back. "Oh, yes. Sorry. I almost forgot."

I then watched as the paper got shuffled between offices and, with more required signatures on it, it then arrived at computers to be input.

I waited patiently outside the cubicles to see that the paper made it to its next destination. It, however, kept getting misplaced. It missed another signature when the person left for lunch, and they couldn't find my file again. Next, no one could find the personal belongings they had locked up when I got there.

This comedy of errors went on and on for over four hours!

I had called my father to come and pick me up, and I knew there was a window of time for my release. Otherwise I would be there another night and that would likely get complicated as my positive energy was subsiding.

After some assistants saw me standing around in my red shirt they said, "You can go to the main entrance, but you will not be able to leave the facility until they find your things. You need to sign that you received them." People had been sent to the storage area to retrieve my things at least five times that day, and every time they came back empty handed.

Finally, the buzzer of freedom was pushed at the nurse's station and I walked out of the ward. I walked to the front entrance of the maze I had been living in for almost two weeks. I went right past the receptionist who was informing me again that they were still looking for my bags and encouraging me to wait.

I had another agenda and continued past her, straight to the glass door where I pushed it open with the last burst of my energy to avoid another hitch in the plan.

I stepped outside of the building and walked as fast as I could to the street corner, then turned to walk down the sidewalk where I hid by some bushes until I saw my father driving up in my car. Only then did I jump up and into the car that would be driving me away from all that had been.

At last I was free!

CHAPTER TWENTY-ONE

I T WAS A LONG drive back to Scottsdale with my father, who chastised me. "Well, Lori, this time you really did it! You have the whole family up in arms about what happened. What the hell is going on with you?"

I danced around his questions during the two-hour drive and somehow managed not to give any answers along the way. The GPS system was playing havoc with me, as the tones and vibrations were piercing through my ears. Finally I reached my limit. I pushed the EJECT button, pulled out the CD that held all the GPS navigation information on it, and stuffed it in the glovebox.

I was starting to feel as though I was going to pay a price for getting out of the mental health facility. There were going to be consequences. The negative energies had me exactly where Oscar and the other brujos said the energies wanted me: insane.

I did my best to appear normal until my father dropped me off at home. Then I worked all night trying to move the negative energies that had followed me home until I collapsed in the entryway.

The next morning, I started to pack a suitcase, thinking that my only way out was to leave, but the energy kept
swirling around me like a vortex. My mind and body were
captive to the task of clearing the space for my survival. I fell
deeper and deeper into the pool of negative energies until it
was too late and I could not get out.

Out of nowhere my shamanic instincts kicked in.
Before I knew it, I was again in for a battle for my life. The
energy in the kitchen was intolerable, so I unplugged all the
appliances. After that, I could hear the hum of energy coming from the other rooms in the house so I went room to
room disconnecting anything that emitted electrical energy.

Then I started a fire, like the brujos did in Colombia,
and I worked on sending individual spirits into the blaze.
The house was swirling with spirits, and they did not feel
like good ones.

I was amazed that I had built-in knowledge of what
I should do. It was as if it had been loaded onto the "hard
drive" of my memory. The shaman in me was emerging with
all the experiences of being a shaman in the past lives that I
had before. One of the methods I used to protect myself was
to create an intricate system of mirrors placed in strategic
areas of my house to direct energy away from me. Even as I
continued working, the energy kept building in the house
until it began to feel like I was inside a pressure cooker.

Next, I took a copper and marble statue of the shaman
that I had bought and placed it on the kitchen island with my
Bible and other objects to create a powerful altar. The rosary
I wore to Colombia was around my neck. Once this was
built, I started commanding the entities to leave my home.

Suddenly, a lightning bolt came crashing down through
the skylight above the kitchen island and into the shaman
statue. At that exact moment the Bible went flying off the

island and landed across the room. I was then pushed violently into the wall behind me and my head was smashed into the drywall. My body slid slowly down to the floor.

Slumped on the floor, I perceived the reality of what was happening to me. It was truly an all-out assault. When I saw the broken marble shaman on the island I knew that I had more than a little problem. My energetic enemies were powerful, so maybe I was just in way over my head. I knew, however, that I had to fight until the end. I could not run from myself.

I got up off the floor angrily, at the end of my spiritual rope. A force greater than me had taken my whole being over, yet I was standing with a determination greater than any I had experienced before. Whoever was behind this scheme was not going to beat me. I had spent six months already battling darkness and the battle was not going to end with my body injured or in a coffin. No way!

I had an innate knowledge to call in the helping, high-vibrational spirits from the North, South, East, and West. I brought in the power of the jaguars, the eagles, the condors, the snakes, and a multitude of other creatures that came to my mind. I called upon every Mayan spirit who was powerful and ready to help me, to come into the space.

After calling in my allies, I went into my small guest bathroom and shut the door. I could hear and feel the vibration of the house rising and rising as if the building was going to explode. For twenty minutes, I sat in the darkness of my bathroom while the energy outside its door continued to build. The whole house was vibrating despite there being absolutely no electricity on, as I had disconnected everything. Meanwhile, I sat and waited. The door to the bathroom seemed as if it was going to bend from the sound and pressure coming against it. But I just sat there, firmly and confidently.

I powered up my mind and body by praying and eliminating my last ounce of fear, knowing that any ounce of doubt would leave me dead. Then I opened a small window on the far side of the bathroom. I had a plan. The door pulsated, the house pulsated, and my head pulsated. When I felt that the house was about to explode with me in it, I said a final prayer, swung open the door to the bathroom, and turned on the light simultaneously, and as I did, a whirling tunnel of energy went funneling past me out of the small window and into the street beyond. It felt like I was in the middle of a hurricane that was passing through my house. The energy that went by me was so powerful I felt it could have taken everything in my bathroom with it, including the tiles on the wall!

I waited a few minutes for the last of the energy to settle and dissipate outside the window. Then I stood up and shut the window tightly. I calmly turned out the bathroom light and walked back into the darkness of the house.

There was total silence in my ears as I stood in my living room. I went over to pick up the broken shaman statue and held it in my hands, thanking all the spirits who had come to help me during the fight. I was barefoot in a blue and yellow summer dress, with the same old haircut I had given myself when I was attacked a few weeks before. The house seemed to be clearing. I started running water out of all the faucets so there would be an energetic flow of purity and cleansing.

The energy continued to dissipate in the house and I walked outside to the patio. I sat on the outdoor couch and looked up to the night sky as quiet and gentle voices came through, caressing me with their words of kindness and concern. I felt cradled in the energy of the good spirits around me. I recognized the energy of the Mayans who were helping me. Theirs were the voices that always took me to safety.

I looked to the sky and saw lights coming toward my house silently. The same triangles I had seen before were now dancing in my back yard. I did not feel threatened in any way by them. To the contrary, I felt like I was being saved and taken away. I looked at the light beams as they began moving back and forth on the grass, like the grand opening of a new movie, and there was so much softness and calm. These were the same lights I had seen at the lake before the beam of light had jolted me.

I had no energy left. My eyes closed as I lay on the outdoor sofa under a curvy mesquite tree and fell asleep.

Hours later I "awoke" to realize I was having another of many out-of-body experiences and found myself standing at a distance from my body in my garden. I looked back at the patio as a team of paramedics rushed to the couch where my body lay. I guess a neighbor had seen me there and found me nonresponsive when he called to me. He had phoned 911. Red lights were flashing on my face as I watched the paramedics frantically pull out their equipment. I was quiet and observed from my position in the garden as they tried to revive me.

I had a momentary internal conflict about whether or not to return to my body and survive, but the moment I contemplated going back to my body I was immediately sucked inside it.

The paramedics kept massaging my chest and screaming at me until the frantic feeling around me began to seep into my cells. I started to feel afraid, which was completely opposite to the tranquility of the garden. Back in my body, I sat up and glanced past the sea of uniformed men to the garden, wishing I was still there.

"It took us a long time to revive you, ma'am. Are you okay?" one of the paramedics asked. Then a multitude of questions started: "Have you been drinking? Taking drugs?" and so on.

"No, no, no," I replied to all their questions.

They then said, "We're going to take a look around in your house." I put my head down, as I knew that seeing my house would bring a whole new set of questions from them that could not be properly answered.

They returned to the patio. "Ma'am, your house is a mess. It has candles, cans of sterno in the fireplace, and you have unplugged everything. Can you tell us what happened in there tonight?"

I lifted my head and said, "No, sir. I have no recollection of how I got here or what happened in my home." Of course, after hearing that comment, they brought in detectives to see if I had been assaulted, raped, or whatever.

I asked them to leave me alone, saying that I did not want to go to the hospital, but the paramedics said that because it took such a long time to revive me, by law they had to take me to the emergency room. They also wanted to eliminate the possibility that a crime had been committed. I climbed on their gurney and they wheeled me past the melted candles and burned-out sterno cans, my broken shaman statue, my Bible, which was drowning in the running water, the mirrors, and the cut cords on all the appliances. I went through the front door to the ambulance that was waiting, and there I was again—being put back into the medical system.

As I lay in the back of the ambulance, I looked out of the window, begging for Tino to help me from wherever he was. When I saw the looks on all the faces of the paramedics who had come to help me, I knew all they could see was a woman who was completely crazy.

Back at the hospital, I asked for an MRI of my brain and for them to do tests for alcohol and drugs, as being intoxicated or stoned was going to be the first thing my family was going to accuse me of. I wanted proof of my sobriety. Sure enough, the test results showed nothing in my system in either of the hospitals. I honestly would have loved a diagnosis of a big fat brain tumor at this point, as it would have made it so much easier to explain all that was happening to me to others.

My father came to see me and the encounter did not go well. Reflecting back on the drive home with me the day before, when I had appeared more or less normal, I understood that he must have been very confused. All my life I had been his model child—first a perfect student and then a big success. I had never been in any big trouble growing up. I was on the honor roll and had graduated on time from college. Then I became a pillar of society and an excellent businessperson. He was very proud of my career and life. My father and I had always been very close and I loved him very much, but my behavior was putting miles of distance between us.

How would I explain to my father what had happened since I got home? I did not want him to see me in the state I was in. I was living from ambulance to ambulance and looking crazier by the day. He was satisfied after talking with the nursing staff that I would be moved to another mental health facility and left the hospital only after much insisting on that outcome.

The soft and gentle voices came back as I was lying on a bed in the emergency room, and I let them have it. "Look at me! How in the hell did I get here? I am probably going back to the mental hospital, and if so, who is going to get me out this time?"

The voices tried to calm me down. "We are going to get you out of here. Don't worry."

"Yeah, right," I said. "How are you going to pull that off?"

They said, "Just do what we tell you and you will get out."

Since I had already been flagged as a roaring lunatic on all the hospital clipboards, I had nothing to lose. I did what they told me. Just like at the lake house after the light beam hit, I felt a spirit merge into my body. I remembered to go slowly so as not to miss a step. I got up and closed the curtains around me, which went well considering that I was hooked up to all kinds of machines. One by one "we" pulled off the cables that connected me to the monitors.

I was sure someone was going to come running in and stop me, but there were no beeps and no sounds that would raise an alarm, and I was still alone.

After we completely disconnected me, "our" hands reached down for my bag of clothes and "we" started to get dressed. Finally, I was sitting peacefully on the bed and ready to go. The spirits told me that I was to think I was invisible and no one could see me, which I did. In a few minutes, they said, "Perfect! You are invisible and ready to go now." They then told me to walk out from behind the curtain into the hallway, turn left, and head for the door where the emergency vehicles had dropped me off.

I took a leisurely stroll down the hallway. I did not lock eyes with anyone and instead confidently headed for the door. For all intents and purposes, I was invisible. I had no idea what I was going to do when I got there because my house was quite a few miles away. I did not have a car or any money, and it was late at night. Still I kept moving.

I reached the end of the hall and the voices told me to stand there a moment, which I did. Suddenly all the lights in the hospital went out and the voices said, "There you go! You can walk out. Go, go! It's time to leave."

But I stood rooted in shock. I could not believe that "my guys" had blown out the electricity to a few city blocks so I could make a dash for the exit. People were running around and nurses were trying to deal with all the machines, which would keep beeping until the generator came on. I felt like I was in the middle of a warped disco as the emergency lights were flashing and the halls were dark.

Before I could make my big getaway, a nurse came up to me as I was standing in the middle of the hallway debating whether to make a run for it or stay, and asked, "You are a patient, aren't you?"

I said, "Yes, but I am being discharged." (Which was true depending on which voices you listened to.)

"Well, now is not the time to leave," the nurse said. "You need to wait until the lights come back on." She then escorted me back to my room. I had missed my opportunity to flee.

Hours later I was back in the ambulance on my way to another mental health facility. As I peered out the back windows, beautiful displays of light followed me. It almost seemed angelic and it did bring me peace during the journey there, but when I reached the mental health facility I was devastated to be incarcerated again.

It was all about the same game plan, process groups, creative sessions, talks about alcoholism and drugs, and more. No one ever mentioned the possibility of evil spirits. I thought about blaming everything I did on drinking too much wine, but there was not enough wine in my local supermarket to get me to this level of craziness and the tests were negative. So I bided my time, did not ruffle any feathers, attended all of the meetings, and followed the rules.

In what would be the last few days of my second stay at the mental ward, the angels brought me a new friend, Chris, who had attempted suicide about a month earlier on the heels of a bad breakup and was doing better now. We hit it off immediately and started to plan a mutual exit strategy. My condition had been stabilized by drugs, yet there was concern that my lithium levels were off the chart and not going down, so they wanted to keep me there. Chris, however, had figured out the system after realizing that if we promised to check into a private place that would address our rehabilitation, we would be discharged sooner. So I followed her game plan.

Together we played all the cards right. Her assistant found a rehab center in California that was perfect for us. I did not check anything about it; I was just going where she was going: out. The transfer papers were signed, and in two days I was released with the understanding that I would go straight to the airport.

As I drove to the airport to catch a flight, I knew I had a chance at ending up in a safe environment offering me some supervised meds, a place where hopefully I could find someone spiritually mature enough to hear my story. My time there would also give me a chance to conduct some research on the internet, do inner work, and sort out what my next steps would be.

As I was waiting at the Phoenix airport for my flight to Los Angeles, I called Deborah to tell her I had gotten out a second time. As I often did, I started this conversation by saying, "Deborah, you are not going to believe this."

There was a funny laugh on the other end of the phone, and then she said, "Lori, after everything I have been through with you, I believe EVERYTHING is possible! You couldn't make all this up if you tried!"

While Deborah and I were chatting, I espied a Native American gift shop across from the restaurant where I was sitting and headed over to buy sage, cedar, palo santo, and every other spirit-repelling herb and item I could find. Still on the phone with me, Deborah was very doubtful that the items would ever make it into my room at the rehab center. Nonetheless, I shoved them in my carry-on.

I was picked up at the airport in L.A. and brought to a beautiful home overlooking the Pacific Ocean. Someone grabbed my bags, which went in one direction, as I was hustled off in another one. I was getting settled in my room when they brought all of my suitcases minus my shaman-ic stuff, which they had confiscated just as Deborah had warned me they would. I was only left with my pouch of protective rocks.

The next morning, I walked into the kitchen for break-fast and the chef dropped some pans on the floor. With staff chasing after me, the crashing sounds sent me running for the balcony, where I almost jumped off. This got everyone's attention. Obviously I was suffering from PTSD, therefore they revised the plan for my treatment.

In the daily group sessions I attended, everyone shared addiction stories and I was shocked to learn about all the pre-scription drugs people were addicted to. Living in El Salvador I had never even heard the names of some of these drugs.

Every few days I would meet one on one with a thera-pist. When I first walked into her office I was pleased to see that she had a lot of crystals and spiritual items on display. I decided to try telling her a "light" version of events. After she got a small taste of what had happened to me, she agreed that we would focus on my trauma for a while.

The overwhelming trauma of the spiritual attack and the multitude of things that happened to me in El Salvador had taken its toll. In a strange way I was relieved that the label of PTSD provided a logical explanation for what was wrong with me. In the rehab house, I felt safe for the first time in a long time. It did me a lot of good to unplug there from the massive energy that had consumed me. Having people around me and daily therapy sessions kept me grounded. This time there would be no missing of any medicines.

After a month of quiet, one day I ventured outside and sat in the garden full of lavender and rosemary. This was a peaceful place where I had already spent hours in meditation and contemplation. I wanted to know what was next for me. I was no longer the same person I had been before Tino's death.

The fragrant air and the flowers engaged my senses. The feel of it made me see that a new reality full of great possibilities was being presented to me, like a piece of ripe fruit, even though I was hesitant to bite into it. After a brief moment of joy, I started to cry and feel sorry for myself.

Tino swooped in. I could sense tenderness in his presence. Even in death I could count on him to show up when I really needed him. He tried to get me to focus on a nearby squirrel, which I did. As I intently watched the squirrel frantically trying to organize its acorns, Tino made a joke. He said, "Nuts."

At first I didn't get it. "What? What about the nuts?" Finally I realized he was making a joke about me *being* nuts. I started to laugh hysterically. I looked across the lavender and could see his face. He was laughing to himself.

At the end of six weeks, I checked myself out of the rehab center and went home to Scottsdale.

Normality remained elusive to me. I was continuing to have sporadic out-of-body experiences, and it proved harder and harder to come back each time. It was crucial to find someone with shamanic training who could help me learn to balance the energy surrounding me and teach me sound principles of physical grounding.

I also felt that I needed to continue with the purification that was done in Colombia, so I called Oscar again. He taught me about creating sacred spaces by placing salt around windows and cut lemons in corners, burning sage, palo santo, and candles, and bathing with essential oils, mug wort, and various other mystical potions. I became a frequent customer at a local botanical shop where I could procure items from Oscar's list of oils and herbs for the alchemical formulas he suggested to heal me.

I dumped over my body bucket after bucket of potions I had steeped on the stove. I was an obedient servant to the process, as I wanted to achieve the same crystalline state of clarity I'd had when I left Colombia. I knew that without a full clearing of my energy field I could not live a peaceful life.

For balance, it was now time for sweet baths. I boiled water and placed sticks of cinnamon and the finest sugar I could find in it, then mixed the water together with flowers, basil, and other herbs, as well as drops of sandalwood essential oil. For weeks I poured this mixture over myself twice a day. It glided like silk over my skin and the sweetness of the potion was ever so welcome.

By this time, I had lost fifty pounds and I felt like I was finding my new self. A different person was emerging as my sorrow melted away. I cast every fear aside, because by doing this I felt assured that I was going to survive. After six months of following the advice I got from Oscar, Marilyn, and Deborah, I was whole again.

I explored the internet to find out all I could about the process of awakening. Surely I was not the only one to have had strange experiences? My spirit guides told me that I was part of a larger process that was occurring on the planet. All of humanity was coming into the wholeness of our being by moving into a fifth-dimensional space with a more refined vibration that allows individuals to recognize their divine essence.

The third dimension, where we are, is the physical dimension. The fourth is an awakening realm, a place of transformation. But the fifth dimension is where we are all headed now. I was experiencing an interdimensional expansion of my soul. As I read other people's descriptions of the process of evolution that humanity was undergoing, I recognized it, as if I already had an inner blueprint of the higher dimensions.

In my research I stumbled on a Mayan symbol that captivated me: the symbol of the *hunab ku,* or galactic butterfly. In the ancient Mayan tongue, *hunab* means "one state of being" and *ku* means "God." The hunab ku is an intelligent energy that pervades the entire universe. It is the architect of life, representing absolute being and the universal dynamism that pulsates and motivates life in its total manifestation of spirit and matter.

The symbol was reminiscent of the *yin/yang* circle from China because it contains both darkness and light in balance. And I knew it was significant to me in some way, as no other symbol held such a profound connection. I sensed it represented the source from which all energy originates.

The spirits impressed upon me that hunab ku lies deep at the center of the Milky Way and transmits radiant energy through stars, which are like lenses to the planets. Earth receives galactic information from the hunab ku via a language of codes, numbers, and energy.

After doing my limited research, I came to the conclusion that the spiritual voices I was hearing were my Mayan ancestors, who had come to teach me the ways of the shaman and to prepare me to be enlightened to the knowledge I already held within my cosmic being. These were invaluable lessons about the thread of separation between light and dark, and the tightrope I was walking between them. The ancient Mayans saw butterflies as ancestors who had returned to Earth to bring them wisdom.

When I asked Tino about the hunab ku, the term was not recognizable to him although the concept of it was. He mentioned that the beauty of the place in which he was then residing was that it enabled you to see yourself for who you are. The healing energy there flows from its source through the soul. This flow is perfect; there is no right or wrong in it. Tino explained that the light from this source is always reflecting through us. Tino said that he would call it God and that souls use this energy, much like a GPS, to navigate to their place in heaven.

CHAPTER TWENTY-TWO

BECAUSE OF THE CONCERN and confusion my behavior had caused among friends and family, I appeased them and continued my therapy as an outpatient at a psychiatric clinic in Scottsdale. It was frustrating, however, that my only option was to seek help from those who saw my transformation through a traditional lens, approaching it purely as an illness that required antipsychotic medication. I took home the prescriptions they gave me and threw them away.

In my therapy sessions, my therapist and I worked on my memories from childhood, which perhaps were the cause of what we were calling now a *psychic break*. My past was analyzed, session after session, in an effort to find the root cause of my obvious misunderstanding of the world around me.

Eventually I tried to convince my therapist that when I was born I had come as a vessel through which there was a large opening to the spiritual realm. I had the ability to hear and see things beyond the physical world. In my innocence, I had felt it was okay to share the things I saw with others. Many spirits came to visit me and I innocently talked with them telepathically and had loving relationships with them. These secret friends would hang out with me, as well as sit on chairs around the dining room table. They were a major part of my life. But when one of my siblings or parents attempted to sit where my friends were, I would scream at them. This caused a continuing disruption in the family.

As a child, I had not realized that the things I was able to perceive would be looked at with great skepticism. Time passed and because neither my parents nor my teachers were spiritually aware, there was no one in my life to validate what I was seeing. Instead I was often reprimanded for imagining things. In this way, eventually I was trained to keep my insights to myself. Basically I underwent a process of cultural indoctrination.

As a child I was comfortable alone and preferred talking to animals and imaginary friends more than to people. I was much more attuned to other realms of existence, because a part of me was always connected to nonphysical energies. Perceiving the world differently caused me to have a feeling of separation from others. Those around me couldn't accept my version of things, so little by little my loving and natural gifts were put to sleep. In time, all my imaginary friends were gone.

I longed for my friends to return and often would sit and stare out my bedroom window, wondering where they had gone. One night, in the quiet of the darkness, a purple star appeared in the distance. I looked with wonder as it moved toward me and then entered the bathroom through a small window. As I stood there, the entire room was bathed in purple light! This was similar to the experience in Napa.

Throughout I kept this sweet and gentle memory a secret, never speaking about it with anyone until I was in therapy. Through my therapy sessions, I came to understand that because I had to give up such a big part of myself to become more like everybody else I had felt I needed things to fill the void. When toys no longer served me, my next move involved possessing the right friends, and then the right job so I could achieve a satisfactory social status. This made it imperative to belong and fit in. I felt the need to attach myself to others and to groups, where I could be a part of something greater than myself. My life became all about ambition, success, and achievement. This would be the package I constructed around my soul.

Explaining all this to my therapist felt good until I shared that I was currently getting spiritual information. Then I noticed my therapist's skeptical smile. Even so, I went on to explain things that I learned from spirits. The spirits' version of my life history was that when I was born a "time bomb" had been set inside me that would go off when I was ready to be reconnected with the shaman within me. I was part of a group of human beings born with a heightened sense of awareness and the powerful gift of telepathic communication. Those who house the soul of a shaman usually only come to embrace their gifts after many years of struggling to understand and accept the responsibilities associated with them. Being a shaman is a difficult life path since there are so many stigmas associated with it.

The therapist listened and made notes about my thoughts, but I did not seem to be convincing her of my mystical point of view. I obediently attended the daily sessions, but I knew that appeasing others would have to stop. I needed to examine my actions through a spiritual microscope in order to arrive at a true understanding of what had occurred when I was under attack. I had to remove myself from a mainstream medical view, which could offer me no accurate physical or mental explanations for anything I had experienced.

I made an appointment with the head psychiatrist of the clinic to discuss my needs and it was obvious when we met that he had spent considerable time studying my case. A very large folder filled an impressive space between the doctor's arm and his body as he arrived for our session. He pulled a chair next to mine and settled into a comfortable position for an understanding talk. "Okay, Lori," he said, "I have seen cases like this where the only explanation is that which is not seen by the human eye. I believe you when you say these things happened. I even checked on the events that occurred the night you were taken to the hospital when you say the lights went out. Because the stories concur, I do not believe you are making this up."

The doctor went on to explain that sometimes there is a thin line between a spiritual awakening and a psychotic break, and although people in his profession struggle with this line, he admitted that many of the events which take place can be validated by witnesses. As we talked about this fuzzy piece of the psyche that could be defined in unconventional ways I was thrilled. Finally someone in a shirt and tie believed me!

I asked the doctor what I should do. "Where should I go to seek answers?" He said, "Why not call the Deepak Chopra Center? They can teach you meditation so you can go inside yourself for the answers you seek. I think we have done all we can do for you. Your next step is the journey to find out who you are now and what all this means for you. Good luck, Lori. I hope you find what you're looking for."

I felt a tremendous sense of freedom. I had finally found the yellow brick road and could leave behind a psychiatric approach to my questionable reality.

The next day I called the Chopra Center and learned it was fully booked for the immediate future. Their staff suggested I call Sarah McLean, a meditation instructor who lived in Sedona, to see if she was available to point me in the right direction. I called Sarah and she was very kind and helpful in recommending some shamanic experts whom she felt would be capable of sorting out more of the details of my journey. One of her suggestions was to go to a treatment center nearby, known as the Sanctuary. I made reservations to stay there for a few days.

I drove to the Sanctuary. After turning off the main road, I traveled down a dirt road sparsely populated with cactus and sage brush. The treatment center was remote and I had a strong feeling it was the right place for me to go. I arrived and walked down the stairs to the center patio where a bouncy blond, former New York lawyer-turned shaman greeted me. Kelley had spent years studying with Peruvian shamans and had an extensive knowledge of healing and divination. She agreed to work with me, taking a contemporary approach to shamanic skills.

Sarah had also recommended another woman to me whose name was, of course, Maya. Kelley knew Maya and told me she would be happy to have Maya come out to the Sanctuary and work with me too.

The following day I waited for Maya's arrival. I smiled at my businesslike formality in such an informal moment as I pulled out a PowerPoint presentation with pictures of the beams of light, the rainbows, and some of the other phenomena that had occurred. I also had a picture of the hunab ku. Maya arrived and walked into the circular ceremony room where we were sitting on the floor. Before she sat down she said, "So, Lori, what's with the four jaguars that were following me down the road while I was driving here?"

Stunned, I asked, "You saw four jaguars?"

"Yes. What is all that about?"

I just smiled, continuing to love that I was receiving verification of my own sense of reality.

I showed Maya the photographs and explained a little about the beam of light that had struck me, as well as the subsequent events. Then I showed her the hunab ku symbol and asked her what it meant to her. With a big smile on her face, Maya stood up and turned around, lifting her tee-shirt above the back waistline of her jeans, asking, "Is this what you're talking about?" She had a tattoo of the hunab ku on her back!

Maya read my eyes like a book, insisting that I was a powerful person with an amazing spiritual gift. But she suggested that I was not embracing it. Instead it was consuming me. She told me to bask in the gift and become it. My main obstacle, as she saw it, was that I was afraid of my power. She suggested that I was confusing power with ego and worrying that after my ego was destroyed—which happens during awakening—I would not feel powerful.

Maya added that I also needed to embrace the power of the feminine. I was not really sure what that meant, but I listened intently to her advice nonetheless, as I was very tired of being beaten up by spiritual energies. She said that it was time to start breathing in power and healing my body from the wrath of scorched energies I had suffered.

Maya's strength was contagious as she taught me to embrace my psychic gifts. She helped me flip the switch, saying, "Remember, this is a premeditated journey, an initiation, and it is time to embark upon it. Everything that has happened was part of the process. When the veil drops between dimensions, a shaman must cross over the bridge. That crossing is what you've been resisting.

"I know you want all the answers, Lori. Just believe and the answers will come. You have been chosen and you will have an impact on humanity, so get over it. Just accept it and live it. Realize that in your power you can be too powerful for some, so they will be fearful. Others will embrace you. There is no deadline here. This is a process. Coming into the knowing has been the hard part so far, but after the knowing comes the healing and the organizing of your spiritual practice."

She advised me, "Gather tools for the protection of your own space. Carry your own bag of medicine around in case you go somewhere you are not sure about. Honor who you are.

"Make altars. Become and embrace who you are. Do not doubt. The power is within you. It is freedom for you to know the truth. Remember the jaguars. Call them in for your protection."

I felt these were words of wisdom and I took them all to heart.

After Maya left, Kelley guided me on a shamanic journey to learn to seek answers from the spirit world. I immediately took off into many dimensions, meeting spiritual guides. Everything I saw was about purification and love and compassion. There was no darkness where I went.

After a few more days with Kelley, I asked her the question I was asking everyone. "Why did all of this happen to me?"

She simply smiled. "Lori, many of us have been chosen to be here at this time—which is why we are switching on. The future does not exist. It is what the energy brings that will take us to the moment. Don't dwell on these matters, as the accumulation of energy will define the moment at the right time. Look beyond the beam of light that you received and find the gift."

I wrote down every word Kelley spoke, hoping that someday I would understand what it meant.

I left the Sanctuary with renewed optimism, although I must admit that at the time I did not understand all that had been shared with me. After checking out, I decided to stay in Sedona for a few more days.

All was going well with my first steps into spiritual rehab, but I was still concerned about my physical condition. My body still felt "fried." My nerve endings were raw, my muscles were compromised, and my connective tissues ached. As a result, I sought the help of Andrew, a prominent energy healer Maya had recommended who was a master of sacred geometry and the infusion of priceless oils from exotic lands into the human body. It would simply have been too complicated to approach a regular doctor and describe the light beam incident. Although I had contemplated telling an M.D. I got hit by lightning, there seemed to be a high risk involved in not being truthful. I might receive an inaccurate diagnosis and inappropriate treatment. Logically, an unconventional experience required unconventional healing methods.

About an hour before the session I called Andrew to confirm that the appointment was still on. He said yes, then asked, "Are you expecting someone to join you?"

After replying, "No, why?" he told me that a special healer had spontaneously appeared at his home and was waiting for me. When I got to Andrew's house, I said hello to Andrew and observed a tall Navajo man with long, dark hair standing near the doorway. I tried to keep the startled look off my face as Andrew introduced us and we shook hands.

The Navajo man, Living Stone, walked very quietly across the floor. Every move he made was done with so
much softness that his reverence for the air he was moving
through was perceptible. He stretched out a beautiful Navajo
rug on the floor and proceeded to unpack his medicine kit.
There was sage, water, feathers, and a round silver container
with a flat lid that seemed to emanate a benevolent force. I
could sense that it was the most sacred object he had with
him, as Living Stone was ever so careful with its position
and place.

Andrew explained that Living Stone had driven several
hours to be present with me and that conducting this ceremony was a rare gift. Living Stone motioned to the rug for
me to sit down, which I did. He started singing gentle songs
in his own language. I felt every melody and word penetrating my cells and softening the effect of my tumultuous
memories on me. He looked at me very lovingly and said, "I
have come here to heal you." At that moment I remembered
what the Mayans had told me they would do: They had sent
me my healer.

Living Stone pulled tobacco out of his bag and rolled
it into a cigarette. He told me he had walked almost a day
to find it in an area inside a canyon where his ancestors had
grown it. Then he lit the tobacco and started puffing on it. I
don't smoke, so I hesitated when he passed it my way, asking,
"Are you sure this is necessary?"

He nodded. "You do not have to smoke the whole
thing. This is sacred tobacco for healing you. Inhale it into
your body and keep the smoke there as long as you can."

I did as he asked, inhaling deeply several times, until he
nodded that it was enough.

Next came hot tea made with peyote. I had heard about
the hallucinogenic effects of peyote so I put up the palm of

my hand to say that I would pass on it. He assured me that it was just a light tea and I would have no reaction to it. I felt very comfortable in his presence, so I took a few sips from the teacup and all was fine.

Living Stone then raised an eagle feather, which he had inherited from his great great grandfather, the Navajo medicine man who had passed all his healing knowledge down to Living Stone. Living Stone dipped the feather in the soaked sage water and tapped it all over my body with soft words that trickled off his tongue. Each drop that touched me sent a gush of cleansing energy through my veins. I closed my eyes to take it all in.

Several times I held gratitude to the Mayan spirits for sending me this man, as I knew they were supporting me in surrendering to the process.

There was softer humming. Then Living Stone picked up the silver container that I sensed contained generations of healing knowledge and spiritual medicine. He took off the cap and told me to touch the material that was inside. It was a black stone, like obsidian, so I touched it with my fingers. Then he signaled me to tap it all over my body, which I did. The flow of energy from the stone made me feel like a soft blanket was enveloping me. I took several deep breaths and sighed over and over in relief.

After about an hour of doing ceremony, Living Stone signaled to Andrew that the healing was complete. He carefully stowed his things, then moved the rug to the corner of the room where he lay down and went to sleep. I looked over at Andrew in total disbelief at what had just happened. He simply smiled and told me again what an extraordinary gift the ceremony was.

Heading to my car I realized that for the first time in a long time absolutely nothing in my body hurt. Nothing. I was completely free of pain. The healing I had received was beyond anything I had expected.

The next day, I headed for the famous Chapel of the Holy Cross in Sedona, which sits high over a red rock canyon, intending to offer up a prayer of thanks for the healing. As I was walking toward the chapel, however, I sank up to my knees into an invisible field of energy that felt like wet cement. I could not move. I was stranded on the path and could no longer put one foot in front of the other. It was bizarre. When I tried stepping backward there was no problem, but there was no way to go forward. Finally, I went into reverse and sat on a bench while all the tourists were on their way to visit the chapel. I was dumbfounded by the strange phenomenon.

After that incident I decided to make an appointment with a local psychic specializing in past-life regression to get help to understand this incident. She described a scene in a past life that related to my instant paralysis: Centuries earlier, I had been severely persecuted by Catholics in Spain during the Inquisition. Something I had done had been misrepresented as animal worship.

The images of what occurred were horrific. A great injustice had been done to me. Apparently, I was placed in an intolerable state of confinement and brutally burned for conspiracy. To exorcise me of demons, I was tortured by priests. I had a vision of myself sitting in a cell with a leaded-glass window. I was in a tower-like building, which was cold and damp, and felt very afraid. A plate of food near me was full of chicken fat.

Something about me had been a threat to those living behind the closed doors of the Church, and I sensed pure evil in the minds of these religious men. This completely explained why, on a quiet walk to a church, all of this had spontaneously entered my consciousness and I energetically sank as if into cement. It also explained why I had recently started to despise eating chicken and why I would at times experience a strange smell of burning flesh. It was another reason for my contempt for what the Spanish had done to the indigenous peoples of the Americas.

The more information I had, the better I felt. After gaining knowledge of these facts and receiving the kind and gentle healing from Living Stone, I drove home to Scottsdale feeling I would be fine. I had turned another corner.

I went home and sat on the patio that night with the automatic sprinklers wetting the perfectly groomed landscape around me. I was missing Lake Ilopango. It still held me in its arms. There was a warm and enveloping feeling whenever I thought about it. As much as I was trying to assimilate into life in the United States, I could not forget the dense jungle and the sparkling waters of the lake. The attachment I had to the lake was real. I decided to go back to El Salvador and start over again.

CHAPTER TWENTY-THREE

Footsie and I went home to Lake Ilopango. My other two cats transitioned during my stay in the United States. Toe died from kidney failure and Canela was bit by a dog. I had sent the dogs home several months before us. In my carry-on the day we traveled were the few things I had acquired since starting down my path of discovery: my drum, various crystals and stones I used for protection, a rattle, my two macaw feathers, and some rocks. All these little pieces of my tumultuous journey were now objects for the altar I planned to build. The TSA guys at the security gate were amused. During my flight I had a bittersweet recognition that August was again at hand, which would mark the second anniversary of Tino's death.

It felt good to return to the lake. Embracing my gifts now, I had arrived with a renewed sense of optimism. The dripping green of El Salvador's rainy season was a stark change of scenery from the hot desert. Nearing Joya Grande, I caught my first glance of the lake that still held the reflections of so many of my dreams there. The glimpse of a fisherman standing in his dugout canoe gracefully paddling, gliding his boat across the smooth surface, calmed any anxiety I had about returning as we got closer to the house.

The doors to the driveway flew wide open, and Maria and Carmen were standing there, hoping that this time I would stay put for a while. Bruno and Baco were happy to see me. As usual Baco barked and jumped on my back and Bruno rubbed my thighs. I embraced everyone and promised myself that I would start over and see this place from a new perspective.

Being home again, I realized that my heart and my soul were still tied to the lake. It was the place where Tino and I lived and where my love for him remained deep. That evening with the soft and gentle waves caressing the peninsula from all sides, the dogs slept in the green grass, never wanting to be enclosed in the house. Footsie was elated to see Maria and Carmen too as he pranced right to the kitchen where there would be no inconsistencies in the timing of his meals anymore. We were all the custodians of this sacred place and leaving had put a heavy burden on our souls. We all held the heartbeat of Lake Ilopango.

Despite the many downpours during the rainy season, the delicate frangipani flowers were intact and added a splash of color to the property. The ring of bright yellow *copa de oro* that I had planted all around the property was spilling over the retaining walls and displaying its bright golden cups of sunshine. It was heavenly to be back.

As I walked with the dogs toward the edge of the property, internally I could still hear the many parties Tino and I had hosted. I managed a smile when I could also hear the lyrics of the Latin love songs that reflected our mood on so many romantic evenings. Tino had such a huge passion for living, and I was so grateful to him for sweeping me into his arms way back when and bringing me to this place that held so much of who I was.

My next morning there, I walked to the driveway. The tree that Tino had died under was dying. I sat in the place he left this world and he softly came into my space. This time I saw his feet, both perfectly intact standing in front of my feet. Tino spoke with a sense of compassion when he said, "There is a light in everyone here."

Tino then became quiet and I could feel the sense of the love we shared. "I have always loved sharing everything I am with you. I am so grateful to have the opportunity to share all that I know now from this new place. I know that we will both find a greater love knowing our perspectives of each other's world."

I asked if he relied on other souls.

"Part of my learning has been seeing beings here that were a part of my life," he replied. "There are many here that I helped during my life, but I have also met others on whom I turned my back. There are family members here too, however our relationships are not the same. We do not have the same roles we had before, though our earthly experiences are still a basis for learning. I still hang out with old friends, as the memories of our times together still draw us together. There are also spirit guides who help direct the learning process through the vast information that is available to us as a part of the transition process from the Earth plane.

"There are beautiful cities in heaven, Lori, that one could marvel at for an eternity, because nothing grows old. I can show them to you. You will see all of these things when you transition. Here is the ultimate destination for human souls."

I so much wanted to see what he was seeing. Was there a way to see this place with my own eyes? I considered the idea that through a shamanic perspective this place might be discovered by me. I knew I would search for that possibility.

He then said, "Lori, be yourself. Be who you are. Stop trying to please everyone in your family and mine. Watching you do this is driving me crazy. Also, be content with what you have and rejoice in the way things are. When you realize that there is nothing missing, then the whole world belongs to you. The first duty of love is to listen and to risk being changed.

"We must come to grips with the inequity of our situation: you there and me here. We must learn to value love wherever it is. Love is the greatest and most dear gift you can receive from me now. Please just look at where you are now and trust that you are not alone and never will be."

I stood up and was taken by how clear our conversation had been without going through Deborah. I looked at the decaying tree again and told Edgardo to cut it down. I did not want to see any more suffering in the driveway.

I looked at the lake as it rippled in the wind and I could not help reflecting on the first time Tino had taken me to Lake Ilopango. We had gone to his cousin's house on the other side of the lake. I was sitting on the patio and saw him hop into his cousin's boat. Then he waved at me to hop in too, and go for a ride. I insisted on waterskiing, which I love to do. I managed to hold on to the line until I let myself fall into the waters of a lovely cove that seemed far away from civilization. I shouted to Tino, "This place is amazing!" while looking at the peninsula jutting out into the lake. As the boat swirled around to retrieve me, Tino enthusiastically replied, "Glad you like it, because it is ours!"

My memories lingered and my familiar deep sadness at the loss of Tino seeped in again until I felt a spiritual kick in the ass from him, impressing upon me that it was time to stop looking back. I sensed he too could see the memory in my mind. We were both moving forward together and it was time now to soar with a passion for life just like he did. I had to let all that had touched me to change me, and move on.

I thanked Tino for catching me before I fell again into despair and then turned to walk back toward the house with a deep love and appreciation for Maria and Carmen and the rest of the staff who kept the property shining. Their faces still held the deep-seated essence of the Mayan. There was a strong attachment in their very cells to this land. I sat on the patio and my thoughts turned to the Spaniards who had come here and treated the native people as ignorant savages. To this day, they would never come to know all that connected the indigenous people to this place.

Now I understood that every rock, tree, and creature had life and a spirit. How could I have walked this land for so long knowing so little? Yes, I had a piece of paper that said I owned this place, but it really wasn't mine. My real wealth was here in nature and in the smiles of those who borrowed this place temporarily with me to walk among the spirits of the land.

Evening came and the dogs were lying on the grass that Edgardo would always mow to a perfect carpet. Although I was merely a custodian of this sacred place, having to leave here someday would be a heavy burden on my soul.

I had always pondered my place in the universe. Every day that I meditated, I felt that I got smaller and smaller and the universe got bigger and bigger. I had started to see the world from the perspective of being in outer space. From this perspective, I recognized I was vulnerable. By accepting and sharing my vulnerability, compassion from others would come. I was not necessarily strong, but I was powerful.

Reconnecting with my soul, I could finally leave the shackles of society behind and travel my own journey. There was no reason to relive the past. I could now pick and choose the people who were the jewels in my life and go forward with them into my future. Of course there will always be the loss of "friends," but those casualties would only bring me closer to those who were worthy.

I began also to lighten my view of what was going on around me. I was sure now that coincidences did not exist. I had lost the feeling that time was running out because I knew we have always existed. I was confident that I had spent many lifetimes on Earth. All these personalities and people were accumulated inside me, making me who I was.

Spending hours and hours in deep meditation was finally bringing me face to face with my inner self and the essential flow of universal energy, which was vital to the cleansing of my soul. All the experiences I'd undergone had taken me to an inner place of nonresistance, where simply existing was enough.

I had lived in and out of higher realms for months. So that I could communicate better with the spirit world and align with astrological changes, I made frequent adjustments to my internal frequency. After all the meditation I was doing, I was able to skillfully attune myself to different vibrational levels. In this period, I was realizing that different spirits had distinct vibrations. This helped me to figure out, by process of elimination, who was speaking to me. I could now better determine whether the spirits interacting with me had good or bad intentions. Many had not made the journey to the other side successfully and remained trapped in this dimension. Some had the potential to create chaos in my mind.

In addition to learning to be discerning in my choice of spiritual friends, I was tapping into my inner voice and strengthening my relationship with all that was within me. Being at the lake in the midst of the elements of nature was an elixir of wellness for my soul. Tino was right: When I grasped nature's potential for healing, I was significantly better.

I wanted to know more about the shaman in me. Otherwise, why was I awakened to this? By now I figured out that I had inherited this identity from a past life. But what did it mean now in the context of my contemporary lifestyle?

I went to my spirit guides for answers and they shared with me that because my soul came innately knowing the skills of a shaman, events had forced me to confront and integrate this gift. Having been born under the influence of the jaguar spirits, it had been inevitable that I would eventually encounter a series of lessons structured to teach me the process of integration. The plan was that I would embrace the jaguar *medicine*—characteristics of an animal that shamans can use for the purpose of healing humans—by undergoing an initiation that would help me to absorb the medicine. Because jaguars have no predators in their natural habitat, jaguar medicine is particularly useful for walking fearlessly through the world.

My path of awakening came with the expectation that it would bring with it chaotic events. Those events would force me to go within myself and discover the mystery of it. It had been necessary to sort through the chaos and endure painful lessons in order to attain clarity about my path and develop higher vision.

There were many roles I anticipated being called to fill in time: spiritual advisor, teacher, and sage—and even silent body of light. But in order to function and honor these different roles, it was imperative to open my ability to communicate freely with the spirits of ancestors, whether that meant seeing into the future or channeling knowledge from the other side. It would also be essential that I embrace the ability to see, feel, and hear things most other people cannot.

Only by owning and expressing the abilities I had been gifted with could I fulfill my assignment, one I had agreed to prior to arriving in physical form.

To be a healer, the ultimate goal was to trust myself and the universal forces. I realized that I could achieve that by isolating my mind. It was imperative that I create my own medicine to heal myself before I try to heal others. The journey I was on required that I learn all about the equal parts of darkness and light, joy and pain, bitter and sweet. Although it seemed these elements were opposites, in reality they were two halves that constituted a whole. The experience of both elements of each pair was necessary for my evolution.

When traveling through other dimensions, the concept of 50/50 balance became the basis for understanding how to live. The universe always conspires to put everything into balance with its opposite. Within the energy matrix everything is balancing, so when I felt energy pushing me one way, I learned to seek complementary energy to push me in the opposite direction.

Whenever I was out of balance, fear and doubt would set in. I would find myself fighting energy rather than existing in it. The messages from the universe were very clear, yet I had formerly missed them because I had been taught to think, feel, and see in ways that could not incorporate them.

The chaos and the craziness of all that happened to me was all part of a master plan put in place by my own soul. The emotional traumas I had experienced were brought about by my own unconscious effort to avoid the changes that my soul recognized were inevitable. When I understood this tendency and learned to "go with the flow" I began to emerge into the light of conscious awareness and become a teacher of the beauty of the unfolding of the soul. My psyche was preprogrammed for this transformation.

The soul plan was to drive myself to physical, mental, and emotional exhaustion until I reached a breaking point. After I burned myself to the ground, I would rise like a phoenix in a new form and with new eyes, transitioning into a new cycle of life that would be waiting for me.

Once I became aware that one type of existence did not negate the other, any illusion of separation between different dimensions dissolved. My four protective jaguar spirit guides, with their beautiful black coats were teaching me the medicine of integration. After integration, this ability of blending in could be passed along to others like me who were ready to embark on new journeys in their lives.

My role in the universe was for my ears to be like the ears of the jaguar, able to hear the voices and drums of the ancestors so that I could help humanity in some way.

I had been a good student of all who were working with me both human and spirit. I knew I was moving beyond myself when I reached the point of not judging anything. I held no self-righteousness. Inspired, I then experienced the wholeness of integration of so many enlightening principles.

The challenge the past year had been that I was taken beyond what my physical senses could process. To continue, I would need to see whatever I would see and not question my sanity. I needed to be steadfast in my goal of retrieving knowledge and bringing it back to the human dimension whole, without my mind or body somehow becoming fragmented.

I knew that I could have never known these things unless I had traveled to the brink of human sanity. With this in mind, I would be able to speak of these things to others with greater clarity.

These were the reasons I was given by my spiritual guides for my experiences. Although I made plans to stay at the lake so I could start new projects, the main project ended up being me. I was relieved to know that I had the power to fix things by just being rather than doing. While seated in meditation I would reach into the core of my heart and send love to all those I had hurt with my confusing behaviors.

I continued my sessions with Deborah, who was now in full swing as my mentor. She was brilliant and carefully taught me what she knew—always giving me just enough to ponder. Never overwhelming me.

The lessons of balance were a major part of my education. I dug deep into the principles of possibility and attraction. It seemed important to allow energy matching whatever I desired in my life to flow out of me so that it could manifest more of itself and return. With my eyes closed, I worked hard on this process and was delighted when I would open my eyes to see the hummingbirds I had manifested at my window.

I learned about forgiveness and that the easiest solution was surrendering everything to the universe. Total abandonment of what I was clinging to would bring me peace. It finally came to me that I did not need anyone to forgive me. What the universe really required for its balance was that I forgive myself. The biggest surprise was that it was much more difficult for me to forgive myself than to forgive others.

Footsie was always by my side during my meditations, basking in the energy emanating from me when I worked with the field of energy that connects everything. Sometimes he would start rolling around the floor or lie spread-eagled on top of my stomach, aiming to soak up the energy.

Life was calm now that I was tapped into source.

CHAPTER TWENTY-FOUR

I HAD MADE THE DECISION to go to Peru, one of the few remaining places where there are practicing indigenous shamans, although their way of life was dramatically fading. When the Spaniards came to Peru, the soldiers chased the native Incas from their villages. Those who survived the onslaught either escaped to the peaks of the Andes or into the Amazon jungles. The shamans who fled were able to maintain their traditions and practice their form of medicine, which many of their descendants still do to this day.

Peru is where most seekers go to understand the world of the shaman. The guide on my journey would be the visionary author Gregg Braden. With my four guardian jaguars spiritually in tow, I arrived in Cusco.

Leaving the airport, the group boarded a bus that would take us to the Sacred Valley, a narrow piece of land tucked between the majestic mountains of the Andes that were reaching up to the sky on both sides. As the bus went turn by turn down the side of the mountain into the valley, I sensed I was going deeper and deeper into a womb. This was the place where I would meet Pachamama, or Mother Earth, and come to know the feminine energy that Maya had alluded to back at the Sanctuary.

After much-needed rest, I woke up the next morning and opened my window to the face of a curious llama peering in at me from outside. I glanced again at the towering mountains above me and understood the escape of the shamans and why the Spanish horses could never reach them in those spires hiding from foreign aggression.

We visited many Incan sites, where Gregg explained the history and meaning of all of the artifacts that remained as a witness to the often hidden messages those ancient ancestors left for our era of humanity to find.

I walked through the Sacred Valley and stopped by one of the many channels of water that had been constructed by the Incas to nurture the abundant harvests that sustained them. The rivers were like umbilical cords, ready to nourish the seeds of corn that would soon be planted. I had taken this walk with the local guide that Gregg had hired to accompany our tour. This wonderful Incan man stretched his arms out across the vast soil and said, "Welcome to the womb of Pachamama, Lori!"

I gazed at the turned-up soil, rich and fertile, and realized I was indeed standing inside the belly of the Great Mother. The nature of the feminine energy that I had not understood in Sedona was now becoming clear to me as I was experiencing the delicate and gentle forces of the natural world that is our mother in so many ways. When I thought of the corn, I felt the seed of life and the cycle of everything.

My thoughts turned to Tino and how, unlike me, he was born into an amazing indigenous world that nurtured and respected life in all its forms, from the smallest kernel of corn to the greatest steaming volcano. I reflected on the cycle of life again and realized its evidence was everywhere.

I knew then that Tino's passing was truly part of a much bigger picture of the continuing process of life leading to death and the journey in between.

That night after our group of around forty people had retired I went out to walk in the valley's darkness. I had just bought a new app for my iPad that shows the location of the planets when held up to the sky. As I raised my iPad, the stars were glittering between the darkness of the mountains and the words *Milky Way* suddenly glowed back at me from the tiny screen! I was now making the connection that the belly of Pachamama was a perfect reflection of the Milky Way above!

I recalled the Mayan spirits trying to explain the energy of the Milky Way as a source of nourishment, like breast milk, for those of us here on Earth. I stood there, alone in darkness, feeling close to this source energy, the hunab ku. I was beginning to understand the reason I had been led to Peru.

The next day was my birthday and I was excited to spend it traveling through the mountains to the ancient site of Machu Picchu. In the early morning hours, we arrived at the park. Gregg had arranged for us to do a meditation there. As the group gathered in a corner of the ruins with special significance, Gregg shared his thoughts about how this place was bubbling with feminine energy.

I chose to be in the back of the group, and leaned against a giant stone where, looking out to a mountain across from me, I watched it pulsating with a very deep vibration, until that vibration was also permeating me. I listened as Gregg described what he was feeling, and as every word came flowing into my soul I felt the strong realization that there was much more to me than just being human.

The land held me. I had come to Peru for more than sightseeing. I was led there to embrace a transitional process my soul had been guiding me toward for over fifty years! I stood in awe of where I was and who I was. I was no longer the person that Lori had been. There, standing tall at the top of Machu Picchu, nothing was left of the old me! Tears were streaming down my face as there was nothing in me to stop their flow.

I left the group and stumbled to a quiet corner where I curled over into my knees and asked the spirits to come to me and help me fully absorb why I was there and what it meant for my future.

A kind and gentle Indian spirit appeared and I wrote down her words.

> *I cannot tell you if your day is beginning or ending, as you live in infinity. The secret of the secret is inside of you. Although life enlivens us it is not the source. The source comes here to you in the Sacred Valley, so you will know the energy of the feminine. Here is the power of your protection. You were brought here to become powerful, to know the powers that exist in this place, by being here. Trust in the knowing of these things. Fear blinds you and only by stepping into the unknown can you find the confidence in the life you will live from now on.*
>
> *Stand on the top of the stones. Draw the energy of your being from this place. Feel deep down in the soles of your feet for the roots of your ancestors, their connection to the Sacred and the Divine. From here you are nourished in the wisdom of the Feminine and bask in the light from the source, the hunab ku, which resides at the center of the Milky Way. Here you are the point of balance, a thin line of particles that connects the dark with the light. This is where you will*

make your home.

Pachamama was holding me in her arms and my soul was ready to be planted into her soft and nutritious body. "Happy birthday," the guides said softly, and then, just as quietly as they had come, they were gone, lifting themselves back into the mountain's mysteries.

As I walked through the ruins of Machu Picchu, I felt truly blessed by my awareness of the corn seed as the embryo of life, the Sacred Valley as the womb of Pachamama, and the Milky Way as the source of my energetic being.

I arrived back at the hotel, still heavy in the experience of the morning. After dinner and dancing with some Incas and receiving a special birthday gift of a small Incan statue from Gregg and his wife, Martha, I went back to my room and Tino swooped in. He wouldn't have wanted to miss my birthday. There was still the physical loss of him and it honestly hurt that he was not with me. It was even more frustrating because I could still not fully grasp his existence. It was asking a lot, of course, to comprehend everything about evolution and the ways of the universe and the spiritual world.

Tino chimed in, "Why do you feel so entitled to know these things? There is no way having such information could ever satisfy your hunger to understand. Even with the fulfillment of your many questions, you will always be at a deficit and never fully comprehending that which is."

He continued, "You cannot measure the longing of the heart, for example, nor describe it. The beauty that surrounds you could never be described. Living things are connected, true, but it is more glorious than what you seek. Lori, you do not know what it is to be a fish swimming in the sea or what an eagle truly feels with his wings upon the wind. If we knew everything, what would there be to seek or look forward to?

"There can never be a time of fulfillment of all the wisdom in the universe. The true essence of it must be touched and tasted. Poets have tried to explain that which is of the heart, just as famous chefs have tried to explain that which they taste. Even so, the ones who dine upon the greatest creations do not find the truth in the way they had expected, because the universe is always greater than our hopes."

I was grateful for the message, but like a dog with a bone I would continue to gnaw at it with curiosity. I was frustrated to contemplate the possibility that what I was seeking was not possible to know. How could he be so sure that a road map didn't exist?

After the tour concluded, I packed my suitcases and headed back to the Lake Ilopango. Reflecting on the lessons I had learned recently, I knew it was important to move beyond the institutions of my previous world. One of the most important things I had learned in Peru was that only those who remain congruent with the energy of the land will prosper. I now had a different view of the natural world around me. Even though my mind kept kicking and screaming for answers from Tino, how could he truly explain his existence to me?

I was still here on Earth, not there with Tino. And while here, there is nothing more important to those who are attached to the land than the land itself. Deep inside it is the vibration that flows through the lifeblood of our bodies like a great spiritual mother. It was important to embrace the feminine power of Pachamama as the cradle of my soul.

CHAPTER TWENTY-FIVE

I HAD ARRIVED HOME WITH a greater connection to my spirit companions. The wisdom they had shared with me in
Peru and the sensory experiences that I had there penetrated
my heart, mind, and intuition deeply.

When I woke up the next day, Maria was very excited
to tell me that a beautiful green parrot had shown up while
I was away and was eating out of Edgardo's hands. It had decided to make its home with us. I smiled at Pachamama and
sprinkled sacred tobacco near the parrot's nest as an offering
to the spirits who had brought us this remarkable gift.

I called Deborah and was excited to tell her all about
my trip to Peru. I told her that the time had come for me
to meet her in person. We coordinated my visit to her in
Virginia in such a way that I could meet Marilyn as well.
Waiting in the hotel lobby for her to arrive, I thought back
on everything she had done for me. Deborah had been the
voice of spiritual wisdom in some of the darkest moments of
my life. I felt so much love and appreciation for her.

Deborah walked into the lobby and the whole place
glowed with her presence. Her delighted smile stretched

from ear to ear. If I could have, I would have picked her up and spun her around, or even thrown her up in the air and caught her, so great was my excitement at seeing her. We kept hugging all the way to her car, laughing and joking, which was always our way of raising the vibration of the energy around us. We were then on our way to meet with Marilyn at her house, where they had prepared special shamanic training sessions for me.

Marilyn was tall and strikingly beautiful, as well as a bundle of compassion. She also had a quirky sense of humor that I enjoyed. Her colorful scarves and fun socks, and her home, rich with an eclectic collection of art and other objects, completed the picture of her uniqueness.

Marilyn was not a weekend shaman. She lived the role 24/7, journeying into the spirit world every morning to seek counsel from her trusted guides. I marveled at how she relied on the spirits for so many of her life decisions, big and small, and how confident she was in what they had to say. Too many times I questioned what the spirits were telling me. Not so with Marilyn.

So, there I was, in Marilyn's cozy basement room with these two powerful women. Deborah had been meticulous in her effort to clear and prepare the space to hold the highest level of psychic vibration. There were no cutting corners on Deborah's watch when a connection with the spirit world would be made. She had followed the instructions from her guides carefully and I could see that reverence and respect for this work with Deborah was non-negotiable.

These women were true pros who knew the ins and outs of the rules of engagement. Their ability to bounce between different realities at a moment's notice and skillfully impart the message of spirit to me was remarkable. They made the whole connection seamless and natural, and I felt extremely protected in their presence.

There was no book that contained the information I sought. For this reason, and so many others, these two women—willing to share their years of experience—were a true blessing. Their care and concern for me was unconditional, and for the first time I was with people who truly understood everything I had endured. I sighed deeply, knowing that nothing I said, thought, or did was beyond possibility in their minds. I was safe and sank easily into a cozy couch ready to learn all that I could from them.

The rest of the afternoon involved learning about shamans and how they use the spiritual world to interact with spirits. It was imperative to achieve a state of purity and ensure that those who were communicating with me were coming from the highest planes of existence, always with a caring, nurturing agenda for others as well as for me.

We then began drumming, asking for more spirits to join us in the space we had created. Then Deborah spoke. "The animals would like to come, Lori. They ask for your permission."

With my eyes still closed, I said, "Of course."

Deborah then said, "Lori, open your eyes. Look!"

Deborah pointed to the sliding door on the patio, and I looked in amazement as squirrels, chipmunks, and at least a dozen birds were scratching at the window or pounding their beaks against the glass. It was a disco of critters moving around to the energy we had created! I laughed, enjoying it all, but Deborah remained absolutely calm, as if this was her normal.

Through my spiritual eyes I had also sensed a fox around me. My amazement swelled when a fox followed alongside the car as Deborah and I drove to the corner after leaving Marilyn's house in the suburbs of Washington, D.C.

We adjourned for the night and I was very pleased finally to be in the right place for this next part of my journey. I had just completed my first crash course in shamanism. The next morning, we returned to Marilyn's house and took the places that Deborah had prepared for us. The altar was full of Mayan offerings I had brought from El Salvador, as requested by the spirits. Copal, corn, sugar cane, and a variety of herbs and spices were added to the small fire. A beautiful cloth near the fire held all the treasured offerings, including Marilyn's medicine bundle and Deborah's most treasured gifts from the Lakota Sioux and other spiritual beings. Sage lingered in the air and the energy felt clear and light.

It then became very quiet. I was told that we would now go to the spirit world and seek the answers to the multitude of questions that I had. I sat in front of the altar across from Deborah and felt a large cat around my legs. It was a jaguar, patrolling the space, keeping watch. Then there was smoke, even though by then the fire of incense and copal had been extinguished. The entire room shifted and in a moment we were all on the spiritual plane of Lake Ilopango!

We started to move back in time and surprisingly arrived at the moment Tino died. The entire scene appeared before me as if I were watching a movie. I watched Tino's head hit the headrest in the car and saw him leave his body. Then, for the first time, I actually saw Tino standing in front of me—looking like a ghost in a Hollywood movie. Initially this was eerie, but then his friendly essence eased the shock of seeing him that way. He was dressed like he was ready to go play golf and was merely stopping by Marilyn's basement on the way to the club. I could have reached out and touched him. Although not exactly solid in form, there was his face, his body, his hands, and his feet, both intact. Seeing all of him standing there finally removed all doubt that it was really him that I'd been speaking to for so many months.

The next day we were back at Marilyn's and Deborah brought in an apprentice to support her. She asked me and Marilyn to leave the space since she and her apprentice would be in preparation for hours, setting things up. Marilyn and I were to go into nature and listen to the nature spirits we found there for more instructions. Our spirits had given us a list of things to take with us before we went to a park near an old indigenous settlement.

I listened carefully and pulled a candle from the bag. I waded into the creek that we were sitting next to and propped the candle up between some rocks, then lit it. The spirits then said the lit candle represented the place where they would come from: the fire in the belly of the volcano! Energy from the center of the volcano would be ignited for our ceremony to come forth. As the waters of the creek ran past the candle, it stayed lit, as if to imply that nothing would put out the fire of the Mayan spirits who lived underneath Lake Ilopango.

Deborah was already well into preparing our path to other dimensions by the time we got back to the house, and after a long five minutes she described hearing a crashing sound as several ancient spirits broke energetic and vibrational barriers to come into the space she had prepared for them. The Mayans had arrived!

The scene I saw changed as the energy changed. There in the basement, I could see a temple rising from the land. At the top of a massive staircase was a platform with a golden chair on it and I could see a priest or ruler sitting there. As usual, I only saw the back of his head. He was wearing a headdress and robe woven out of the hyacinth macaw feathers. I glanced over at my blue and yellow feathers sitting on the altar in the real world and smiled.

A multitude of priestly beings gathered around us. The dimensional barrier had been broken, so information began flowing to me freely as I waited for Deborah to take her next step. Deborah seemed somewhat startled at the high levels of the energy that had arrived, but remained very composed and in control. She let it flow through her, speaking on the Mayans' behalf. "We bring information from the universe. Do not underestimate the power of the jaguar," a spirit said. "We are far more advanced in our knowledge than you can believe."

Then a spirit in the form of a serpent appeared, circling around the altar that we had carefully placed in front of us as the interaction began. Deborah said, "Lori, they are trying to make a determination as to who you are. They want to confirm that you are their leader."

The Mayan priests began to circle around me, looking at me, "smelling" me, and trying to verify my identity. Yet honestly, I did not know. I deferred to them, waiting to learn the identity they related to. Deborah reported that during the two hours of preparation earlier that day when Marilyn and I went out, the spirits had required her to lay out some of my clothing that I had left. I continued to sit as those Mayan spirits walked around me.

Eventually, they described me as a new initiate. They said, "You were sacrificed. Why are you alive now? We are surprised you survived the initiation process we started. Now we realize you were not prepared. Now we see that our plan to bring you into the initiation process was too much for you. Our goal was that by opening you to the energies your destiny would bring you back with the priests again. The beam of light was our way to bring you back."

The Mayans continued to circle around my body and my energy.

Deborah seemed to be negotiating with a very important priest who was coming from very high levels to make the final verdict. And another, rather confused priest continued to walk around me. He seemed to have a connection to me from other lifetimes than his cohort did. For the first time in my awakening process I could actually see these spirits as if they were living people standing in front of me—although their appearance was ghostly, faint and translucent, I guess because it had been many centuries since they lived on Earth.

I shifted and felt myself go in reverse to their place and time. I felt jaguar energy lift me into the chair on top of the temple. I was all-powerful and claimed my space, then I began to speak with a forceful and unrelenting voice and demeanor, saying, "How dare you question who I am! You are peering into me as if I am a stranger! That is pure fiction! You all know who I am! I am the power that left you so many years ago, and now I am back, yet you cause me all of this turmoil and suffering? Why are you here? For more suffering? I have been through enough! How dare you question me!"

My human mind was in shock, as the words did not come filtered through it. I gasped at the air, wondering how the sounds had appeared, as the head priest said, "But you are a woman! We are not sure about this." I could sense that they wondered why a woman had been chosen to carry out their cosmic plan.

I raised my hands and started pointing my fingers at all of them, shouting, "What does it matter what body I am in? I still hold the power of the jaguar gods! You are to cease questioning my identity! You will no longer question or doubt me! I am in all of my power and any doubts are to be destroyed."

I then sensed a slight shift back into Lori, but the power was still there when I screamed, "You shot a beam of light into me, almost destroying my life, and now you come here and question who I am?"

I felt my back erect against the same golden chair from my visions, and energetically I was in my full regalia, decorated with many feathers. I sliced my hands across the air and told the Mayan spirits to stop the madness of questioning me. I was their leader and it was enough! I had had enough!

The two women in the room with me were silent as were the spirits of the Mayan priests. I gazed down to my left foot and there was a jaguar by me, alert, but content, as the power resided in me. The scene then started to fade as the priests left. Then it grew quiet.

Deborah was still in trance and far off in another dimension. Her apprentice was energetically holding the space. Marilyn looked awestruck. As I shifted back into the energy that was Lori I continued to be amazed that I had been able to see the faces of the priests and engage in conversation with them as I did. I still felt powerful, and waited for what would come next.

At that point, a Mayan woman began to speak through Deborah. She said:

> There is something indestructible at the center of you
> and while the process has been difficult for you, you
> will see that this is a gift and a blessing. Remember my
> words, there will never be a pain that does not bear a
> blessing. We had to break you out of the earth plane as
> it was covering up who you are. There were too many
> layers keeping you from awakening into this process.

*We had to crack a nut to get to the core of you. The
lake holds secrets that will be uncovered for you.*

*We needed to shift family and friends from you
to make way for others that needed to have room to be
close to you at this time. These new friends will bring
people that you need on your journey. You had become
disconnected to the spirit animal world. We admit that
the energy that was infused in you was overwhelming
and we are doing our best on healing this. We agree
with Marilyn that we must consult with her and her
guides first before moving any great amounts of energy
through you, as we do not have enough experience
doing this through the human form.*

*Our messages are from the cosmos for humanity
and there will be more messages to share. We recognize
the damage to your physical body and emphasize the
need for healing. We remind you of your power, but
temper it and note the distinction of this power from the
power of the ego. We ask that you focus on the humility we have taught you in the knowing of the light and
the dark. When you feel the true essence of the power
you will know your path.*

The woman then sank back into the waters of the lake
and she was gone. The ceremony ended. The validation
of the truth was in the air; it was not just my imagination
anymore. It was now real and something I would need to
understand and accept.

Deborah was back to being Deborah. I asked her what
she thought about the whole scene and she answered, "The
spirits that came knew you were their leader because of what
is housed inside of you. It is like a cosmic locator beacon.
They felt confident they were not mistaken. At first there

seemed to be some doubt that they had chosen the correct energy/human for the awakening process, but you cleared that right up. When you started to speak, I made it clear to them that you were who you were, and they had the right leader. I believe your purpose will soon be revealed to you. We will wait and see what comes."

The next day, I was still almost speechless after what had happened. After the startling session, I had tossed and turned in bed, taking inventory of my new reality. It was true that everything had been stripped away from me: friends, family, my ego, my plans, my persona, my two cats, and my husband. All that had been was no longer. There was a feeling of great loss.

I walked into the coffee shop to meet Deborah with a half-assed plan for changing course in my life. I was frustrated, as it seemed that the more information I obtained the further I moved away from finding the meaning of all of this. Just how long was I going to have to keep searching for the reason why I was hit by the beam of light? *Why is my life all about Mayans?*

I sat down, gripping my coffee cup, and asked Deborah, "Okay, where is the switch to turn this whole thing off?" She replied with a hum and silence, so I asked her again. I knew her hesitation meant the answer was going to fall hard on me.

Finally, Deborah replied, "So let me understand this, Lori. Your husband dies and a rainbow forms over where you put his ashes, not just on that day but exactly a year later. Then you are transformed and inherit an innate knowledge of shamanistic practices. You are clairvoyant, clairsentient, clairaudient, and who knows what else. You walk in and out of your house and drumming starts and stops. Then you get hit by a light beam and now when you see lights you see sacred geometry. One afternoon a cloud shows up and rains only on you . . . but you don't get wet.

Deborah caught her breath, then said, "After all of that, more light beams show up at your bedroom window in Napa Valley and slam into you, resulting in another out-of-body experience."

Her tone remained steady as she continued, "To top it off, you consistently talk to your dead husband. And you are asking me how to turn off a switch?"

I loved Deborah for her brutal honesty; it was always given with my best interests in mind. She concluded, "Lori, there is no going back when you have the gifts you've got, especially after all that you have been through. When those from the spirit world call you, you need to prepare yourself for a different kind of life. Do you honestly think that all these things, which have totally transformed you, mean nothing?"

Okay, so Deborah was right. I needed to accept my destiny, but I also wanted to know what the hell it was. My insatiable mind wanted to know everything.

Trying to fill myself with some humility, I got in Deborah's car to go to the airport for my flight back to El Salvador. I welcomed her loving embrace as we said goodbye. After I turned and walked into the Dulles airport, the tears started to fall. I thought about this most unique relationship I had with Deborah and Marilyn. They had entered my life with quiet footsteps and smiles you could feel and hear even when words were not being spoken. Their presence was magical and they gave me a most precious gift, which was to believe. They showed me that deep in stillness there was always someone watching over me, since spirit was only a breath away.

I would never see most things in the same way as before. The stars now twinkled with the gift of knowing there was the other side. The trees held roots to absorb what I could not handle. A rock would never be just a rock to me, as I now knew it contained consciousness. A crystal was now my protection. This experience, which taught me to revere all things indigenous and spiritual, was now a luminous part of my life, and the heart and soul of my journey. What a magical world I lived in! Birds and squirrels, jaguars and spirits, and most of all the gift of Tino, in all his brilliance and humor—and the knowledge that love lives on far beyond this world—were part of my life now thanks to Marilyn and Deborah.

CHAPTER TWENTY-SIX

A FTER SURVIVING ANOTHER CHRISTMAS without Tino around, New Year's Eve arrived. While I was waiting for the clock to strike midnight, I realized how much of a mistake it was to be anticipating what was next. I stopped myself and let the anticipation of what was next fade into reflections on New Year's Eves past, the first kisses, the clinking of glasses, the noise-makers, and cascading fireworks. For fifty-six years I had been in similar settings waiting for a ball to drop. The fireworks went off. I wondered, *What am I celebrating anyway? The past or the future?* To celebrate either seemed futile to me now. I was simply in a place at a time, and that was all.

As much as I wanted to control my future, I was beginning to realize that it doesn't exist until it occurs. It was essential to stay present. Only what occurs is reality. I could no longer extend the view of my life so far out from me that I would never experience today.

In the weight of the moment, Tino swooped in and joked, "Did anything that you anticipated happening last year happen?" I laughed and said no. "So, what is all the new anticipation about?" he asked. "It is simply a guessing game people play. You all say that life will be different in the New Year, and of course it will. But that's only because things change. This thinking is useless, as no one can know about tomorrow today."

It was New Year 2012, the beginning of the year that the Mayan calendar would end a 25,000-year cycle, and I would have to be patient to know what the months ahead of me would bring.

The spirits emphasized trust. They told me I was now fully capable of healing myself and others by using the vibration of compassion.

This seemed to be a recurring theme in my meditations. It was what the spirit world was hoping we humans would embrace in our worldly existence.

The spirits seemed very confident that each of us would regain the perfection we had when we were born. There was a belief that little by little humanity would learn to manifest more harmoniously over the next few years.

During the year, I softened my view of others. I could see the light behind the eyes of people I met, a light that revealed the soul behind the facade. The spirits often shared their sense of hope that there was no longer a need for hierarchy, and that the world would truly become "flat" in the sense of all of us becoming more compassionate. That itself would destroy the need for structure. We would instead simply care about others so that the need for rules and regulations to ensure that we get along would dissipate. There would be no need for governments and politicians, as without our egos running rampant, we would not feel a need to rule over others. Instead we would all be on the same footing.

The messages I "downloaded" from the spirits were not farfetched; I could feel the truth of them in my bones. It became very clear that things were changing.

I sought the wisdom of a *tata abuelo* ("great grandfather"), an indigenous elder, in El Salvador whom I brought to the lake. We walked out to the point together to the spot where the beam of light hit me. He told me he was aware of an energy portal there. The tata abuelo said this opening was needed to help many ancient souls that were stuck in Lake Ilopango move into a new dimension. A time of rebirth for humanity was coming. It was like we were all being held in a mother's womb, waiting for the next age to arrive. Soon humanity would begin the process of becoming something different in collaboration with other energies. The consciousness of the whole world would shift following a specific event foretold to occur in 2012.

Our meeting sparked my curiosity. In searching the internet for more details, I came upon volumes of writing about 2012, much of it channeled from the spirit world. My group of helper spirits told me to avoid reading such prophecies, as they would dilute the purity of the messages they were sharing with me. They cautioned me not to get confused by all the hype and had a good laugh when I asked them what I should be doing to prepare. Frustrated with my ignorance, they assured me they already had it covered. In fact, they had been working on the details for thousands of years. They told me I should have confidence that with so much time for planning, nothing had been left to chance.

After the holidays, I went back to Scottsdale and started to research a plan for my education in spiritual matters. Deborah and Marilyn suggested that I study with the Foundation for Shamanic Studies. The Foundation had several teachers spread throughout the United States, and I was lucky that one of them resided in Phoenix. I signed up for an introductory course that would be held in late January.

I arrived at my first class not knowing what to expect. What would students of shamanism look like? It was quite a surprise. There were retired health care professionals, a medical doctor, entrepreneurs, college students, and my teacher, who was both a shaman and a registered nurse. Our first assignment was to journey to a different dimension and bring back insight and information.

Surprisingly, the tasks I was asked to do in alternate dimensions came easily to me, as if I had been doing them all my life. I ventured into other worlds and saw things there as if I was on Earth. I clearly heard the spirits and the other entities I met on the way speaking to me. I felt very comfortable in the class and everything resonated with me. I was thrilled to begin to travel to the spirit realms as I was being taught. It was like taking a super freeway after only being able to venture on back roads.

In class, I learned there are three layers outside of the reality we live in. One is the upper world, which is connected to galactic energy and holds the vast dimensions where souls travel. There is also the middle world, which is closest to where we live. Many souls—like the Mayans in the lake—get stuck here when they die because they do not know how to move on, or do not want to. There is then the lower world, which has many beautiful dimensions as well, and holds deep, intense energy from the Earth and connects us to our ancestors.

After taking the class, I was able to travel to these dimensions. So I could find safe passage, I began to map out navigation routes. When I was traveling, I could sense the heartbeat of the hunab ku penetrating the other energies that were guiding me. I felt certain that with this skill I would be able to find the spiritual answers I was seeking for others and myself.

Ready to give it a try, I traveled out into the universe to find Tino. It was not as difficult as I expected. Within minutes, I arrived at the place where he was. Everything there was in perfection as he had described it to me. The scenery was beyond comprehension, and I was happy that he was surrounded by so much beauty. There was joy in the air and nothing was missing; it was complete. *Well, I made it,* I thought to myself, looking at this most marvelous world he was in.

At first, I felt like Peeping Tom in the place as I managed to float in and out of the scene. Tino was standing there in black pants and a white *guayabera,* just like the one he wore at our wedding. Then all of a sudden, I too was dressed as I was that day. He held his hand out and we walked to a bench and sat down.

The scene of the day we got married appeared like a magical backdrop. "Lori, our marriage was one hell of a ride," Tino said. "Being on the Earth I could never come to know about the love that I have come to understand now that I am here.

"I am sorry, Lori, but know that this pain-in-the-ass is learning and asks your forgiveness, as I learn what love really is. Age does not make one wise, but now I know the wealth of wisdom comes with understanding the love that you had for me."

I sat, listening quietly in deep appreciation. It was a massive gift from the spirit world to experience this and hear him say the things that were left unsaid before he moved on.

Tino then took me further up into the upper world and I found myself standing on a beach near a small house. We simply stared at each other, not really knowing what this experience would bring. As my emotions emerged from my heart they flowed toward him, and our two life forces came together in a spiritual dance that felt soothing. There was no feeling of sensuality. I instead sensed the energy of deep, enduring love revolving around us as our energy entwined.

When I was in Tino's presence, my mind could not communicate in a complete way. If I wanted to express myself to Tino, my message had to originate from my heart. I realized that losing my thoughts would be the key to communication. When we had made a connection, my essence and his were caught up together and, like a sail in the wind, we were suddenly flying over the ocean. Sadly, this experience lasted only a brief moment, until my mind intervened and questioned what was happening. Suddenly the scene came to an abrupt halt, and I was back on the beach, alone.

I was no longer in my wedding dress. I was back to me. And I returned to Earth the same way I had left.

Little by little, I was gaining confidence that I could open myself to the spirit world safely. In the past, there was deception. I had often mistaken the identity of the energies that I was working with, but now the vibrational footprint of the spirits who were tapping in to me were familiar. I could now recognize them.

It was early morning in my home office in Scottsdale. I was staring out the window as the sun came up. It had been almost three years since Tino had transitioned. I glanced back at my computer and in my inbox was an email that gave me a sense of urgency. "Death and Dying Conference" was written across the top of the announcement. I read further. A star-studded cast of experts on the topic of dying was coming to Phoenix. I immediately signed up.

The first day of the conference I met the authors of many of the books I had read after Tino died: scientists, doctors, philosophers, psychics, mediums, grief counselors, and more. One of the speakers scheduled for the following day was John Holland, a talented and compassionate psychic medium who performs on stage by doing spontaneous readings for members of his audience. He helps departed souls communicate with the living.

Back home after the first day of the conference, I relaxed on the patio and read through the agenda for the rest of the seminar. I looked up delighted seeing the rabbits heading for home before the neighborhood bobcat started sauntering around. I moved into a deep meditative state and fine-tuned my emotional frequencies with Tino's wherever he was on the other side so we could have a mental chat. I was on a mission. I had a challenge for him. "Tino, tomorrow there is a psychic at this conference. Let's try to pull off an appearance."

I could sense Tino liked the idea. In fact, I felt it excited him. I knew it was a long shot, as I was sure everyone there would also want their own deceased loved ones to appear. But I knew Tino, and if anyone could pull this off from the other side, he would be the one!

The next morning, I found myself changing my outfit three times. Finally I stopped and asked myself why, since normally I was never indecisive about what I wore. This day, my appearance seemed important. I laid out several outfits on my bed and waited. Finally I felt Tino pop in and say, "The turquoise one."

I also put in extra effort with my makeup and gave closer care than usual to the earrings I would wear. After they were on, however, they kept falling out. I picked them up and put them back on, over and over, until I realized Tino was playing games. Then I told him simply to knock it off!

I drove to the event with an air of expectation. I could feel Tino's presence. He seemed playful. As I pulled into the parking lot, I said, "Okay, sweetie, today is the big day!"

Over 300 people were in the auditorium. Choosing a seat toward the back of the room at the end of a row, I waited. Then John Holland came on stage. I sat with confidence, believing Tino would be arriving soon.

John started bringing in spirits for people on the opposite side of the room from me, and I listened carefully as, one by one, loved ones appeared with messages. That particular day there were a lot of children coming through, so I was grateful to the spirits that their parents were being given this opportunity to reconnect with them and resolve any unresolved issues.

It was getting toward the end of the presentation and still no Tino. I began getting a bit concerned that he might disappoint me. John then tapped into another spirit recognized by two women at the end of the row where I was sitting. *He's getting closer,* I thought. The women were having a very emotional encounter with their deceased mother and there were lots of tears. Holland was doing his best, but then he seemed distracted and apologized to the women that another spirit was interrupting him, a spirit named Tino. The two sisters looked at Holland and said they did not know anyone named Tino.

At that same moment I could feel Tino's trademark swooping energy come near me and I felt his agitation that John had not made the connection that he was not with the ladies at the end of the row. I continued listening to John Holland's conversation with them when suddenly my earrings fell out on the floor. As I bent to pick them up, I heard John's voice change with excitement. "Wow! Excuse me, but I really need to acknowledge this spirit named Tino, who is quite insistent and just came flying in here!"

I lifted my head and looked toward the stage, thrilled that we had pulled it off. John continued, "Wow! This guy has an amazing presence! He is tall. His name is Tino, and he is showing me his feet. He says his feet were cut off from diabetes." John then peered into the audience, asking who could connect with this new powerful energy that had arrived. With my earrings in my hand, I rose and lifted my arm as a man quickly brought a microphone. "That would be me," I said.

John's reading continued. "Tino is showing me a huge, impressive ring with diamonds and emeralds. He says it is your wedding ring and you did not put it on today."

I looked down at my finger, and John was right. I was wearing a much simpler ring Tino had bought me as a birthday gift. John then described Tino in a white Cadillac, wearing a golf hat and smoking a cigarette. It was exactly the picture of what Tino looked like when I met him.

Through John, Tino went on to say he had been married three times, but with me he had met his true love in life. He then described in greater detail the toes that had been cut off, and how I had found a blue rubber boot with a perfect seal so that he could go into the swimming pool while his wounds were healing. John said Tino was showing him the place in Central America where we lived together, and he also made it very clear that he never let his physical limitations get in his way. He had always enjoyed life to its fullest.

John commented several times about how funny Tino was. He called him a "real party guy" who was doing his best to describe the pool area with trays of food piled around the edges, and, of course, a full bar. Coconut water, vodka, beer, wine, scotch, tequila, and mixers abounded. No request was left unfulfilled at Tino's bar! John was having fun with Tino and also with me, as I was validating everything he said.

John finished the performance. Walking by me on his way out, he gave me a hug. "That was great! How fun to meet you and Tino and finish my presentation on such a high vibrational note."

Afterward, people were coming up to me to express their thoughts and the fun they had getting to know Tino, too. As usual, Tino was a rock star for everyone just fifteen minutes after meeting him. I returned home ecstatic that Tino and I had pulled it off.

CHAPTER TWENTY-SEVEN

IT WAS NOW JUNE and I had decided to sell the little patio home with the crooked mesquite tree. It did not hold the best memories as we had bought it as a place to stay when Tino was at the Mayo Clinic. It was a constant reminder of his suffering. I walked out of the front door and never looked back. It was time to go back to El Salvador to re-group and jumpstart my future.

On the plane back to El Salvador with Footsie in tow, I was deep in contemplation about my next steps. I felt that this trip would galvanize a conclusion about my life in El Salvador. I had been in the United State for over six months, venturing from one seminar to another to learn everything I could about shamanism, as suggested by Deborah and Marilyn, because I knew I had a date with destiny.

I called Deborah since we were both determined to get to the bottom of what my connection was with the spirits under the lake. Why were they so invested in my life?

In this session, we asked that they show me my rela-tionship to the Mayan people, and then a disturbing ex-planation came. Deborah and I were shown a shockingly violent scene. There was a pervasive smell of burning copal in the air. We were atop the temple I had seen in previous visions for a nighttime ceremony with torches illuminating the darkness. People were lying on their backs on the floor, just before a sacrifice ritual was to begin.

We then saw a hand cut into a human chest and pull a heart out—still beating. To my astonishment, it was me in that Mayan lifetime. I was the one holding that heart in my fist and lifting it high in the air. The hand then swept around me, creating a semicircle of energy. Heat and vibrations emanated from the people around me.

The scene finally, and mercifully, ended!

I now realized why this deep, dark secret had been kept from me as the realization was devastating. Then the spirit of the same woman who had appeared to me at Marilyn's basement came forth again to speak to me. "Your role is to bring the souls you sacrificed into the present. They are stuck in the past due to commitments they made to you and the tribe. They believe they sacrificed themselves for the good of the people, assuring that for generations to come there would be crops and food for all.

"The Mayan priests who are with them now, and who have been trying to reach you, realize now that this was not necessary. Therefore they can no long continue to stay in sacrifice and hold fast to this idea from so many ages past.

"Things are not the same anymore. Now there must be evolution and change. Your task is to lead them out of the old belief. Free them to see clearly again. You were a strong leader and it is important to lead them forward. This is of vital importance to them, and extremely relevant to you as well."

The message went further to explain that I had been "wired" for this purpose—given a lighter frequency that made it easier to shift. My destiny could not be denied. It was only a matter of time before the many events in my life would direct me to confront the Mayan imperative head on.

My soul knew I was born to serve as a conduit between different spiritual realms. My mission would only be realized if I helped others taking their own first steps on a similar journey.

I knew preparations would be made so I could fulfill my obligations. The Mayan ancestors were telling me that because of human sacrifices and the explosion of the caldera roughly a half million souls were under the lake and that I would be called to help move them. Because I carried energy familiar to them, I could convince them it was all right to move on. It seemed that these spirits would not leave their place of being without my involvement.

The spirit of the Mayan woman told me that energies would move through me as the Earth created changes to its own molecular structure. This energy would come from the Earth's core where there is a vast bed of tourmaline rock. It would flow through fissures in the Earth's crust. Of course my human mind was spinning! *How? What? When? Where?*

The spirit guide could hear my thoughts and continued, "You are to release the Mayans from the lake and help them transition to their next place. As their leader, your role is to tell them that this move is the right thing to do and explain that it is their right to leave. They must understand they have the ability and option to do this, and not to hold so tightly to the old promises related to the history of the lake."

I asked this spirit guide if these people always had known I would come back. In reply, she said that for these souls I had never been lost. "The people are connected through their hearts and minds to the essence you carry. You have never been far from them. This is not about a religious coming, like you humans conceive. These spirits believe in an energy actually housed in you. You have never 'not been,' even though through the last hundreds of years you have chosen many other forms.

"These spirits can always reach into you. There is never a place where you are that you cannot be reached, as you are part of their hearts and minds. Beyond any religion, this is a perception and a belief. It is what those people understood as they grew into maturity. It has been their faith and remains the key concept that allows them to exist.

"You must realize that all of those who are on Earth now house within them the many generations of their past," the spirit woman continued. "It is impossible to know the intricacies of your evolution to this point. In this case, there are things these souls remember because your relationship with them has spanned many generations and lifetimes. Because the time that has passed is so vast, we cannot tell you why these people still recognize you. The leadership role that you have with them, however, has never changed. Whether one has been in an exalted position or lived as a humble servant, the form one takes is not important.

"The Mayan priests have always known who you are, although a for a long time they were confused about the form you had taken. You not only affect those below the lake, but many others beyond this lake as well.

"Our message to you now is that you are ready for the task you must accomplish. We will provide all that is necessary for the plan to be successful, since your human mind is not capable of complying with all there is to do. Do not be concerned. Housed within you is everything you need to lead. It has nothing to do with physicality. Even if you are in Scottsdale and never set foot here again, you still house what is Mayan within you.

"Those at the lake looked to you for guidance and assurance that their way of life will continue in the right order of things. They view you as their leader, the spiritual jaguar who interacts with the gods. Divine energy moves through you. You are the intermediary for these people, since you hold a vibration that is still linked to the representation of divine energy that they understand and resonate with. In order for these souls to be part of the coming evolution, they must move."

She concluded, "This process is also important for you, as you must evolve beyond this connection."

With that, the session ended and the Mayan woman left. Deborah simply asked, "Did you get that?" and I said yes and we hung up. I was speechless in the knowing. I numbly walked out to the patio and lay on the chaise longue. The immensity of what I had heard started to trickle into my understanding. All my questions about my purpose began to disappear, even though so much of what was being asked of me was far beyond what I could comprehend. I finally settled on just accepting that I, like so many other beings, was the product of an accumulation of many lives. The only difference was that I was being held to some cosmic accountability for a multitude of souls.

The next day I did a final session with Deborah before the long-awaited shift of energies that would prepare me for what I was to do. Once again we were back on the phone and a young Mayan spirit we did not know came in to help and show us all the holy offerings that were used in the ancient Mayan temples. It was important that I knew how to sanctify what was necessary for the ceremony.

"You, as a high priestess, can do these things," she told me. "But I have also come to assist you."

Priestess? I am now a priestess? I was curious to hear myself being defined that way, but I didn't question it at the time.

"I will be at your side throughout the final ceremony," she continued. "For your ceremony we will bring together the ritual with all the required dignity, so be prepared. We will bring the vibration to its rightful place where the land and the water are connected."

As much as I had tried over the past weeks to process all that I had heard, I had dropped all my resistance to the message and I was ready for whatever would happen. I knew that without this ceremony I would never be free of my Mayan destiny.

Since I housed the familiar energy that they needed to direct them from their existing place under the lake to another dimension, I would utilize the energetic portal that the tata abuelo had identified a few months earlier at the same spot where the light beam hit me. There I could lead them up and out into the cosmos. In this ceremony, I would give them a peek into the world above. They would see blue sky and white clouds through the portal, if only in a small circle of light. This would give them hope where there had been no hope before.

The many spirits Deborah channeled for me explained that a cocktail of energies would come from the rocks, the water, and the land—converging into one energy within me. After this convergence, the Mayans could move away from me into destinies all their own.

I had been instructed to meditate for three to four hours every day prior to the ceremony to establish my connection to these spirits. During these meditations I would go under the lake. The Mayan priests there told me not to speak to anyone; I was simply to walk among the beings. Many souls were not yet willing to leave, but because they trusted me as their leader they started to come around to the idea. My role in leading this journey of release for them was predestined, but my abilities needed to be fine-tuned so I would be in the right state of being to help them through the portal.

When I reflected back on everything that had happened to me to reach this moment, I was amazed. It was hard to imagine that after so many hundreds of years that this multitude of souls would now move through the portal. I would be a bringer of life and an instrument of change as a karmic reward for releasing them from their original sacrifices.

The date with destiny had been set. I was to serve as a healer by receiving energy from universal forces that would shatter negative energies around me and bring everything into a positive state. The Mayans who had sacrificed themselves would then partake of the paradise of the soul. This ceremony would show the world the possibility of beauty. I was to do all of this in remembrance of the sacrifices of the many souls trapped under the lake.

The spirits had told me to start my ceremony by forming a heart connection to the sun and the earth. Father Sun and Mother Earth would be my guides. Then I would bring in the love for me from the spirits at the lake. If I ever doubted my capacity, I was to rely on my heart, which would know what to do, as it had been preparing for generations.

I spent a week working with the young priestess that Deborah was channeling to ensure that all of the details would be in place. I did my best to explain what I was preparing for to Maria and Carmen, and they trusted what I said and seemed to know somewhere in their consciousness that this was an important destiny to fulfill. We carefully made a list of all the things the Mayan priestess had asked for and then Maria went to the central market to buy them:

flowers, sugar, candy, copal, sage, tobacco, and a multitude of other offerings. The day before the ceremony everything was piled onto my desk and Maria smiled over her accomplishment.

I was at ease and calm. I leaned back in my desk chair and glanced over at a vision board I had created a year earlier with the help of the spirits. In the center of it was a white piece of paper reading "My Soul's Goals." These were:

- Freedom.
- Satisfaction that I am making
  a difference in the lives of others.
- Fulfillment of my purpose in being here.

I started to laugh, thinking, *Boy, Lori, you really need to be careful what you put on your vision board from now on!*

The rest of the afternoon I spent time in meditation in the sacred space of my heart, healing the places that had been wounded by my process of awakening to my soul purpose. I was ready.

It was December 21. I'd had a restful night and woke to Maria's knock on my door at four in the morning. I went into my shower and washed myself diligently, scrubbing until I could scrub no more. The smell of sandalwood lingered, its essence permeating me with the knowledge that it had been used in many religious and spiritual traditions to honor their deities.

As the water flowed over my body, my form began to change into a crystallized state and it felt as if I was glowing. Once I'd toweled my body dry, I sat in meditation again, moving into my heart space and sorting out the energies around and within me so I could move ahead most effectively with my sacred task. I applied a drop of sandalwood essential oil to my forehead, neck, and chest as instructed.

The guides had explained that this would help move my energy closer to that of the Divine.

I went into my closet and was guided to wear a shirt I had bought in Guatemala, handmade by a woman in a small Mayan village.

Then I walked down to the point where I would do my ceremony in the darkness with all of my offerings, which I placed on a rug I had brought from the highlands of Peru. As I sat in silence in the darkness and started to cry at the enormity of the moment, the voices came in, "Yes, you weep, and the lake is deep. Rightly so, as many have been deceived by governments and hierarchies. Many tears make deep lakes."

It was still dark, but sunrise was getting close. I took the rocks as I had been instructed and formed a circle with them around the pile of *estacas,* a kind of holy wood soaked in a special liquid the local Mayans used in their ceremonies, which Maria had found at the town's central market. Listening intently to the spirits, I then placed yellow flowers in a circle within the rock circle around the spot where I would build a fire and placed copal, tobacco, rice, beans, corn, and fish all in their proper places related to the four directions inside it. Then I walked around the circle thirteen times with a bowl of burning copal.

There were four bowls of water. One was placed in each of the four directions. I called in the spirits from each direction, as well as Mother Earth and Father Sky. I then stated my purpose to the spirits and placed sugar around the entire space as an offering to myself—as I had been told to do as sweet compensation for all that I had endured to be there. I then reached into the center of the pile I had created with a lit torch, starting the fire. As the sun was now breaking over the horizon, I looked across the lake and saw that it was in a state of perfect calm.

I had now shifted into my role as leader and I could feel my transformation into the feminine energies that I now knew so much about after being in Peru. The Divine Feminine would lead their journey to transition. It was now becoming crystal clear.

Of course! The Feminine has been worshipped as a goddess in every tradition since the beginning of time, except in the modern world. It is the mystical, magical, powerful, primal symbol of Mother Earth, representing balance, healing, renewal, and restoration. The Goddess symbolizes the primary life force on the planet. If we don't utilize the love, nurturing, understanding, and kindness of the Divine Feminine that exists within each one of us, humanity simply won't survive. This essence is needed to restore balance to our world.

I picked up my drum and began singing and pounding it to the rhythm of Mother Earth. The drum's vibration sent reverberations over the water so those beneath it would know that it was me who had come.

After a few minutes, I studied the surface of the lake again and observed ripples of energy moving outward in circles from where I was seated. The fire was massive and getting bigger. I was alone, and I had left instructions for no one to come to find me or watch what I did. The sun continued to rise and the power of the moment was reaching a crescendo. The voices instructed me to send unconditional love from me for the souls at the lake on my drumbeats, which I did.

Soon I began to feel all the souls in the lake moving. They were hurling through the tunnel of energy I had created for them, which was fueled from the volcano that still existed at the base of the lake. I saw the souls begin to go into the sky above me, moving up and away from Earth and throughout our galaxy. Thousands and thousands were passing through the portal that I had opened for them with my drumming and massive bonfire! Watching them go was an experience I will remember forever. These souls were ever so gentle with my body and concerned for my safety as I handled the intricacies of the event.

This time and this place had finally arrived after so many hundreds of years, and I was humbled to have been the catalyst for the change that was required.

Every soul involved left the lake, each finally free to go on. And then, the movement of souls was complete.

I sat by the now less-than-ferocious fire as smoke from it engulfed and swirled around me. I dove into my essence, intoxicated by its power, as it cleared away all the thick energies that had at times overtaken me. There was a massive purge of energy from my body related to all that had just happened.

Finally, I took the last bowl of offerings—veins of tobacco leaves—and threw them into the fire. With this task complete, fresh energy then seeped through my veins into my heart, and gradually spread throughout my light body.

The purification of my soul continued as every cell in my body was cleansed and the energy moved toward my brain. I could sense the headdress of hyacinth macaw feathers on the top of my head as smoke rose and circled around it, finally engulfing the feathers until, in tiny particles, they began to dissipate around me.

I stood up and after one more look at the lake I began to walk back toward the house, leaving the ashes of my bonfire and my Mayan karma to die in that place where the beam of light had struck me so many months before. I was then standing where the car was when Tino had died and a chiltota bird appeared at the perfect time on a branch nearby. I stood there as we both took in the other, with our heads moving side to side in a contemplative dance of curiosity of what might come next.

The young Mayan spirit was still with me as I arrived at the house and Maria, who was full of anxiety about what I was doing, came running to greet me. From a distance she stopped. I waved at her and gave her a thumb-up signal to indicate that everything was fine. I then saw the spirit standing next to Maria. She also waved at me and then merged into Maria's body and was gone. It had been Maria's soul!

I was not surprised that such a kind and beautiful soul resided in Maria, as she had remained so loyal to me through every twist and turn of the journey I was on.

I put my arm around Maria and we walked into the kitchen, where I found Carmen too. "Maria, would you please make me some beans and rice and a tortilla?"

"Sure, *Señora,* whatever you want."

CHAPTER TWENTY-EIGHT

AFTER A MONTH OF rest and reflection, I woke up one day feeling that I needed to make a decision about leaving the lake. Maybe it was time to move on. Yet the lake had been the backdrop of my life for almost thirty years—encompassing my life with Tino before and after his transition. Leaving would be like walking off stage in the middle of a wonderful love story. In some way, I felt that doing so would be betraying us.

I sensed a presence in the bedroom. Tino was sitting in a chair with his head in his hands observing me. "I will be happy if you leave. It is time," he said. "Things have never been the same as when it was just you and me. It is not a good thing that you live here alone." I sensed he had been watching events as they were taking place. "I never envisioned you here alone; it never crossed my mind when I was on Earth."

I closed my eyes with the pain of leaving this Eden behind. "You are right," I said. Then I got up, poured myself a cup of coffee, and went to my computer to make reservations to leave for Arizona.

Later that day, I rode in the boat to the spot where I had scattered Tino's ashes. This time there were no tears, because it no longer felt that it was the only place my husband existed. The boat floated gently next to the rocks as I contemplated what was next. The duck had already moved on. But I let that concern dissipate. For as much as I wanted to make a list of things I could control about my future, by now I realized list-making was futile.

My mind began working like a scavenger going through a mountain of memories of living at the lake with Tino. Memories were important and there was an abundance of them. I would need a forty-foot trailer to take it all with me. I still felt sad about the dreams that would stay behind, but content to know that the memories would come with me.

My last night at the lake, I had a dream that Tino picked me up in an airplane and took me to see more of the world that he lived in on the other side. It was quite a trip. Since he had been a pilot in life, this experience was authentic to me. I was happy and embraced every minute of it. When the trip finished, I slowly opened my eyes to find Tino's hands holding my own. They were as perfect as I remembered them: His long fingers, covered with soft skin, even had the smell of him. It was an identical feeling to the first time he touched me shortly after we met.

Next, a great rush of loving energy poured into me when his arms appeared and cradled me. I turned over so that I was on my back and then I saw all of him lying on top of me. His head dipped down and his lips pressed against my lips and I was completely enveloped in his energy field. The energy started to dissipate as his voice said, "You can never say I did not kiss you goodbye." I lingered in the sensation of the kiss and the gentleness of the moment, and then he was gone. I smiled warmly. There was nothing to say.

Miracles happen.

It was time to leave the lake and my heart was as heavy as the three large suitcases that were crammed into the SUV. I looked at Bruno and Baco and held back the tears because I was leaving them. I also did not want Carmen, Maria, and Edgardo, my family and best friends, to see me in despair about not knowing when I would see them again.

At the airport in El Salvador, my phone rang. It was Maria calling to tell me Baco died in the same spot that Tino took his last breath. I guess he had waited so that the pain of him dying did not add to the mountain of sorrow I was already taking with me. I found a corner in the airport where I sat and drenched myself in tears at the loss of Baco as well as the many people and things I was leaving behind. My world in El Salvador was crumbling and coming to an end.

I arrived in Sedona where I had leased a lovely home on a creek. This was to be a place of healing for me where I could wash away all of my deep emotional pain of leaving.

Every morning I woke up, put my feet on the floor, and realized that I had won the battle. I feared nothing, absolutely nothing, having achieved the ultimate prize of not fearing my own death. The door to life was wide open and I was ready for the business of embracing life because I trusted the universe again. I was in the loving arms of spirit and out of the wreckage, truly safe.

I stuck to my guns and refused to take any of the medicines that were zealously being offered me by mainstream therapists. Instead I was determined to stick to my plan to seek out natural healing with local healers and naturopathic doctors. I was unwinding and emotionally unpacking.

Throughout the spring I spent many contemplative times sitting on the patio by the creek. The barren and twisted branches of wisteria along the roof of the patio were filling fast with delicate purple blooms that were beginning to emerge. I embraced the feeling of transition as every day I would see new buds bursting from the branches.

The day I made my decision to make my home in Sedona, Tino appeared to me seated in a chair across from me on the patio. With a contemplative smile on his face, he said, "Sedona? Well, this could be an interesting choice. A bunch of crazy people live here who talk to the dead."

I broke into hysterical laughter at the thought of the two of us, me a crazy-assed, PTSD-psychic-break nut who could see and hear dead people talking to a crazy-assed dead person. Caught up in this comedy, Tino, who preferred Scottsdale and had always considered Sedona a place full of kooks, also laughed at how ironic it was that we were now here. He faded away after cracking a joke that he never thought he would be caught "dead" in Sedona.

I spent a year building a new home in Sedona. Tino, who was a civil engineer and loved the building process, was of great support. Spirit and Tino moved things along in record time and I was surprised because the day the builder gave me the keys to the house, saying it was finished, was the anniversary of the day Tino died. On a quiet Sunday afternoon after I had settled into my new home in Sedona, my house was suddenly filled with the ancient Mayan spirits. My new puppy, Gracie, was barking and Footsie scuttled under a chair. I sensed the presence of the Mayans and asked, "Why are you here?" They said they had come to share more information about the identity of the soul that resides within me. They knew I had been curious for a long time about my identity in past lives and my ancient connection to those under the lake.

The four jaguars then appeared in my office and took their places in the four directions. They showed me an image of a flying jaguar.

Then one of the spirits spoke. "There is a filing box that you brought from El Salvador. Inside the box is a folder of papers that we asked you to print almost four years ago. Go to the box." I got up from my desk and went to the closet where the box was, whereupon I searched and found a file labeled "Mayan Stuff." I flipped through the papers with the Mayan spirits waiting and was guided by them to pull out a piece of paper that told the legend of a Mayan priestess named Comizahual.

This is a legend told among the Lenca Indians of Latin America, who are the modern descendants of the ancient Mayans, about a priestess of unknown origin who ruled them two hundred years before the first Spanish explorers arrived. The people called her Comizahual or "flying jaguar," after the mighty wildcat that is much feared and respected by the Lenca. Her reign marked a turning point in their ancestors' history.

A woman of great dignity and extraordinary beauty, Comizahual was part of a monarchy from the lineage of the jaguar. Because she possessed the natural gifts of leadership and compassion, she built a stable kingdom through leadership, not war, unifying many opposing tribes. Her people adored her and were happy to obey her regulations. She also was a sorceress and worked wonders using the magical arts.

Comizahual promoted advanced cultural evolution and laws that respected multiculturalism. She also encouraged trade and permitted all forms of religious symbols to be displayed. She dedicated a lot of her time to help the people in the villages near the valley of Managuara. Among other things, she helped people to learn about medicine, weaving, law, astronomy, and calendars. She then built a palace in Cealcoquin, the loveliest and most fertile part of the region.

According to the legend, when Comizahual was dying her body was adorned with bright yellow flowers and she was carried on her bed through the streets on the shoulders of chiefs. When the people saw her, they rushed out of their homes and surrounded her, weeping and asking her blessing. Suddenly a light beam came out of the sky and pulverized her body, which transformed into a multitude of chiltota birds that took flight. Comizahual vanished.

Reading this story with all the spirits standing around me, I couldn't help recalling the bright yellow copa de oro flowers I too had gathered for the ceremony. I was amazed to read of the beam of light that had shot into Comizahual's body, which was just like my experience.

The spirits then reminded me that the first house Tino and I built in El Salvador was on Calle La Chiltota. One of its nicest features was that there were yellow flowers cascading over the garden walls.

I turned to a painting hanging on the wall of my office that I had commissioned an artist to paint without much input from me. She had painted a strong Mayan priestess. An image I now believed represented me in a past lifetime. Yes, I had been the Mayan priest in the headdress who had perished in a hut, but I had also been a priestess named Comizahual. Looking again at the painting, I sensed the power of the now emerging feminine and the strength of who I was and who I am now.

CHAPTER TWENTY-NINE

TWO YEARS HAVE PASSED. It is a Tuesday morning and I am on my patio looking at Elephant Rock, waiting for the sun to reach the top when it will splash through the two-story-tall windows of my new home in Sedona, Arizona. Footsie is hiding among the red-hot poker plants, which provide just enough camouflage for his morning hunt. Gracie brings out her squeaky toy squirrel, shattering the silence and sending the local lizards scrambling, much to Footsie's dismay. My life is "normal" now.

I pick up my coffee cup with a rooster on it and smile. It holds memories of a happy past gone by and my first meal in El Salvador. The coffee, which is rich and smooth, is really the only thing I have left from my life in El Salvador, except for a closet full of photo albums that hold a million memories from the last thirty years.

Now I am a mystic in ordinary reality. In my shamanic medicine cabinet reside many gifts from nature and other healers. Gathered from sacred sites and places, it holds copal, maize, sacred sage, volcanic rocks from Lake Ilopango, holy water from Mother Mary's home in Turkey, sacred water from the *balians* ("spiritual healers") in Bali, a sorcerer's wand found for me in a consignment store by a fellow shaman, red dirt from a medicine wheel in Sedona, crystal grids, the miracle sand of Chimayo, New Mexico, and a crystal heart and piece of jasper from Marilyn. Using such tools I have removed ancient spirits from bedrooms, cleaned up haunted houses, counseled souls on their way to heaven, healed the most chronic of chronic pain, reset unbalanced biochemistries, brought back disconnected pieces of souls, and many times seen the sources of a disease or a mental illness and then sent clients off to their conventional doctors with clues as to what is needed from the western medical arsenal to heal them.

I have found that radical change can result when the natural force of such tools is harnessed by my intention and partnered with universal energy. I can see into the many past lives of my patients and remove the scars of trauma that impede their earthly journey. The process is magical, yes, but it is natural and it has always been available to humanity.

I sip my coffee and reflect on all that has happened since Tino's passing. I still miss his physical presence and I will always cherish the unique relationship that developed between Deborah, Tino, and I. Although a sense of loss prevails, I know that he is moving forward in his evolutionary journey. He is evolving, as am I—and I like who I am now.

When I felt that our vibrational connection had started to diminish, in a deep meditation I went to see him. He no longer resembled the man who walked the Earth. He instead was a cosmic ball of light with the essence of Tino. I could feel an intense love coming from this ball of energy. I stayed and watched it emit purple, blue, and yellow lights. There was no language, only feelings and impressions of the highest vibration. He was all soul, an accumulation of his many lifetimes all rolled into one. He had fully transcended the life experience. I sensed great joy from him when he "spoke."

There is not a sense of loss or longing, where I am, Lori, I am complete. There is not a day not a night, yet darkness forms around me, and I am light. There are no needs. I am form, but I am me. This does not mean I no longer engage with you or others on Earth or that I have abandoned you. It is simply that in order to take this form I had to unchain myself from all that was earthly. It was a challenge, as I wanted to be with all of you, but I knew that I had to go to another level of existence. Here is a place of being and higher thought.

I no longer have earthly love, as there is not enough fullness in it. Where I am, there is a complete fullness of love. It's so intense that when I come near you, I must reduce who I am as the love that I am is too great for you to encounter in your dimension.

Do I have longing for arms and legs? No.

Do I wish I could be there? No.

But I want you to know that me leaving does not in any way diminish our love or my thoughts of you. An eternal flame that remains in me will always know you. This flame can never die, it will always know you wherever you are and can always find you. Nothing exists that can extinguish it. I still see you, your face, and your body. I see your life. I care.

We will always be together, Lori. We have a bond that is deep and wide. You are me, I am you.

Ours is a connection of many lifetimes. We will continue to be together in this one until I see you here. There are no goodbyes. There are no separations with death, as we always find each other. There are no barriers between us, as I have never been lost to you.

Scientific research tells us that if you place two living heart cells from different people in a petri dish, these cells will in time establish and maintain a new, common heartbeat. This biological fact is the secret behind all strong relationships. It is cellular proof that beneath any resistance to connection we might experience, and beyond our attempts at connection that fall short, in the very nature of creation itself there is an essential joining force that brings us all together, which is the hunab ku.

ACKNOWLEDGMENTS

There are many individuals who deserve acknowledgment for their support during the events described in my memoir and for their participation in the preparation of the book.

I am grateful to Deborah Harrigan, who walked beside me all the way, and to Bebe Salinas, Marilyn Hayes, Janet Dobbs, Maya Starhawk, Kelley Alexander, Living Stone, Angelita, Tata Abuelo, Oscar, Farides, and all the brujos and brujas who worked with me in Barrancabermeja, Colombia, for their compassion and spiritual gifts, which were instrumental in helping to bring my inner shaman into the light and love of living.

I am grateful to my Salvadoran family, Maria, Carmen, Edgardo, and Jorge, whose unwavering commitment to my well-being saved my life.

Symbolist Joost Elffers is an alchemist whose style and creative curiosity about me and my journey helped my story into its sacred wardrobe so I could step confidently forward with it into the world. I am grateful to him and also to graphic designer Patricia Childers for making the book beautiful inside and out.

Publishing consultant Stephanie Gunning is a spiritual gatekeeper with keys to the mysteries of the literary kingdom. She has a big jar of fairy dust which she sprinkled all over my manuscripts through her editing and invaluable advice.

My appreciation also extends to Lisa Furgard, who told me I was a good writer, and I believed her; Barbara Mayer, a wisdomkeeper, for her valuable input in the early stages; Sharon Walker, Leigh Henry, Gina Lake, and Nirmala Erway, who read early versions of the manuscript and provided valuable feedback; and Jason Buchholz, who helped me to refine the chapters and bring them into a compelling Mayan melody.

I am grateful to my stepson, Francisco, who never wavered in his support of me; my stepdaughter, Carolina, my granddaughters, Tiffany and Elisa, who ran not walked to my side; my parents, Tom and Donna Morrison, who after all the chaos and confusion embraced me with a lifetime of unconditional love for the new me; and Carlos and Ampy Novoa, who gracefully stepped into my life in the darkest moments.

Thanks to the hundreds of authors whose books I read: Every story gave me a piece of the puzzle of wisdom I was seeking. For those I traveled with to Europe, Latin America, Indonesia, and parts in between, I thank you for being my earthly guides.

These acknowledgments would not be complete if I did not acknowledge my spiritual guides: the four jaguars who walk beside me, the essence of the priestess Comizahual, my lifetime companion the sacred lioness, the council of Mayan elders who work with me tirelessly to help others, the shamans that merge with me so I may be a channel of healing, and many other spirits who lovingly accompany me through my life's curriculum at the University of Earth.

ABOUT THE AUTHOR

Combining her skills as a coach, spiritual counselor, healer, and psychic intuitive, **Lori Morrison** has built a successful practice in Sedona, Arizona, working with clients from all over the world. She has had particular success in supporting those who have experienced trauma, grief, and debilitating life events, and has dedicated herself to the use of alternative methods and ancient wisdom to reduce her clients' reliance on antipsychotic medication.

As a counselor, she is guided by the goal of changing the framework around mental illness from one of despair to the recognition of the emergence of a creative gift that can lead to dramatic improvements in recovery. Lori is a member of the Mental Health Coalition of Verde Valley, Arizona, where she advocates the acceptance of complementary programs for mental illness.

Lori has traveled the world while studying the application of sacred sciences and shamanic and alternative healing methods with many of the world's most recognized spiritual teachers. Her work incorporates a spectrum of new ideas and innovative approaches to balance body and mind.

Prior to the spiritual awakening that led Lori to her work in the spirit world and in mental health, she was a New York banker, a successful wine and gourmet food purveyor in Napa Valley, California, and Central America, and a philanthropist. She is especially proud of her contribution to social and environmental causes around Lake Ilopango through a foundation she established with her late husband, Tino in El Salvador.

Visit Lori at www.LoriMorrison.com